The Household Tips of the Great Writers

The Household Tips
of the Great Writers

MARK CRICK

GRANTA

Granta Publications, 12 Addison Avenue, London w11 4qr

First published in Great Britain by Granta Books 2011

Excepting the preface, the text in this book was previously published with
colour illustrations in three volumes: *Kafka's Soup*, first published by Libri Publications Ltd,
2005, extended paperback edition published by Granta Books 2007; *Sartre's Sink*, published
by Granta Books 2008; *Machiavelli's Lawn*, published by Granta Books 2011.

A CIP catalogue record for this book
is available from the British Library.

1 3 5 7 9 10 8 6 4 2

ISBN 978 1 84708 252 7

Typeset by M Rules
Printed and bound by CPI Group
(UK) Ltd, Croydon, CR0 4YY

Contents

Contents

G<small>REAT</small> W<small>RITERS</small>' DIY T<small>IPS</small>

Contents

GREAT WRITERS IN THE GARDEN

Preface

with Mrs Isabella Beeton

In these days of technology, texts and tweeting it seems there is but little time to spare for homely tasks. While the breaking of lump sugar, the stoning of raisins and a great deal else goes undone, both young and old seem so consumed by the demands of social networking that a good knowledge of household matters has become a rare quality.

The decline, however, is not irreparable. Here is a book that, in combining the craft of literature's greatest talents together with the good sense of the housekeeper's expertise, will not be altogether unwelcome in addressing this worrying state of affairs. And though I cannot approve of all the instructions gathered in its pages, I will acknowledge that in attempting to treat of the house, the kitchen and the garden together in one volume, heart, liver and lungs, as it were, of a single body, the author and his editors have spared neither time nor pains.

Well practised, the arts of the cook, the handyman and the gardener hold the means of immeasurably extending the boundaries of human enjoyments, but I would caution you from falling too readily under the influence of certain contributors.

Whatever the merits of Mr Irvine Welsh's cakes, I cannot, in all honesty, condone the means of their production. To my mind a cook who keeps late hours, conducts his work in a state of intoxication and cares little for the freshness of his ingredients should be avoided as a pestilence.

On the important subject of gardening, where moderate but continued attention should be your aim, I would like to direct you to the examples of Mr Raymond Carver and Mr Pablo Neruda. The story told by the former is a perfect illustration of how slothful ways in the hanging basket can lead to ill-tended relationships in the home, while the musings of the latter, though fragrant, provide a poignant reminder of the perils that await the gardener whose pastime becomes his ruling passion. Mercifully, these are exceptions, and the editors have seen fit to include many accounts by gentlemen and gentlewomen of more moderate temperament.

On this account I wish to acknowledge the valuable contribution of Mr Jean-Paul Sartre. During the last few years great advances have been made in the principles of sanitary knowledge. It has been proved, in an endless number of cases, that bad or defective drainage is as certain to destroy health as the taking of poisons. Mr Sartre's commitment to the subject of blockages is second to none.

A happy house must be a well managed one; its requirements are well within the scope of us all. Under the guidance of teachers such as these, learning them need not be a toil. Let the ruler of every house then rise to the responsibility of its management; and in doing their duty to all around them, may they receive the genuine reward of respect, love and affection!

Great Writers in the Kitchen

Lamb with Dill Sauce

à la Raymond Chandler

1kg lean leg of lamb, cut into large chunks
1 onion, sliced
1 carrot, cut into sticks
1 tablespoon crushed dill seeds, or 3–4 sprigs fresh dill
1 bay leaf
12 peppercorns
½ teaspoon salt
850ml chicken stock
50g butter
1 tablespoon plain flour
1 egg yolk
3 tablespoons cream
2 teaspoons lemon juice

I sipped on my whisky sour, ground out my cigarette on the chopping board and watched a bug trying to crawl out of the basin. I needed a table at Maxim's, a hundred bucks and a gorgeous blonde; what I had was a leg of lamb and no clues.

Lamb with Dill Sauce

I took hold of the joint. It felt cold and damp, like a coroner's handshake. I took out a knife and cut the lamb into pieces. Feeling the blade in my hand I sliced an onion, and before I knew what I was doing a carrot lay in pieces on the slab. None of them moved. I threw the lot into a pan with a bunch of dill stalks, a bay leaf, a handful of peppercorns and a pinch of salt. They had it coming to them, so I covered them with chicken stock and turned up the heat. I wanted them to boil slowly, just about as slowly as anything can boil. An hour and a half and a half-pint of bourbon later they weren't so tough and neither was I. I separated the meat from the vegetables and covered it to keep it moist. The knife was still in my hand but I couldn't hear any sirens.

In this town the grease always rises to the top, so I strained the juice and skimmed off the fat. I added more water and put it back on the heat. It was time to deal with the butter and flour, so I mixed them together into a paste and added it to the stock. There wasn't a whisk, so using my blackjack I beat out any lumps until the paste was smooth. It started to boil, so I let it simmer for two minutes.

I roughed up the egg yolk and cream and mixed in some of the hot sauce before putting the lot back into the pan. I put the squeeze on a lemon and it soon juiced. It was easy. It was much too easy, but I knew if I let the sauce boil the yolk was gonna scramble.

By now I was ready to pour the sauce over the meat and serve, but I wasn't hungry. The blonde hadn't showed. She was smarter than I thought. I went outside to poison myself, with cigarettes and whisky.

Tarragon Eggs

à la Jane Austen

40g butter
4 eggs
Ground pepper
Pinch of salt
2 teaspoons tarragon (fresh or dried)

It is a truth universally acknowledged that eggs, kept for too long, go off. The eggs of Oakley Farm had only recently been settled in the kitchen at Somercote, but already Mrs B—— was planning a meal that would introduce them to the neighbourhood with what she hoped would be universal acceptance. Her eggs had been strongly endowed by nature with a turn for being uniformly agreeable and she hoped to see at least a half-dozen of them make fine matches in the coming week. The arrival of a newcomer in the parish presented the perfect opportunity and Mrs B—— wasted no time in sending out invitations to a luncheon.

Many hours had been spent discussing the merits of one

dish over another with her neighbour, Lady Cumberland. The two ladies took prodigious care when considering the advantages of tea over coffee and whether the toast should be white or brown, subjects on which Lady Cumberland delivered her opinions in so decisive a manner that Mrs B—— dared not disagree. Lady Cumberland was no supporter of the new cooking, which she blamed, first, for bringing ingredients of obscure origin into undue distinction, and secondly, for raising cooks to honours of which their fathers and grandfathers had never dreamt. As a sacrifice to propriety, Mrs B—— agreed that the dish would be a traditional one.

With the day of the luncheon drawing near, Mrs B—— was suffering terribly with her nerves. The event that she had announced with such anticipation had ceased to be a source of pleasure. On the contrary, it was unfair of the local ladies to allow the burden of organising such gatherings to fall so often to her; and was it not strange that Mrs Eliot had not returned the courtesy of the dinner that she had given a fortnight past? Such were the mutterings of Mrs B—— as she paced the garden seeking inspiration, when the sound of a carriage crossing the lawn announced the arrival of Lady Cumberland, who suggested a small rehearsal. So it was that the two neighbours found themselves in the kitchen at Somercote, still busily searching for a proper suitor for the eggs. While Lady Cumberland sat drinking tea, Mrs B—— chose for her employment to search the pantry, stalking the absent suitor.

"Parsley might do," said she. The herb was a regular at the house and the chance that it might combine well with her eggs meant that Mrs B—— could only think well of it: "Good-looking, with an easy and unaffected manner." Lady

Cumberland's reaction was unequivocal: "Too much curl to its leaf, and too often seen in great bunches at fishmongers. It would be a most unhappy connection."

Mrs B—— was not used to disagreeing with the better informed mind of Lady Cumberland, and now, her every cherished opinion of parsley's worth overthrown, she turned her eye to rarer visitors, including the tarragon. She had always thought tarragon a difficult herb and hard to please. "It refuses to grow here, it refuses to grow there, but fancies itself so very great, disappearing every winter I know not where. I quite detest the plant."

"French tarragon is an aristocrat among herbs, and although I think it too good for your eggs, I cannot deny that it would be a fine match for them," said Lady Cumberland. Mrs B—— received the remark with all the forbearance of civility and the slight on her eggs went unremarked. But a recommendation from so high a source as Lady Cumberland could not be ignored, and Mrs B——'s contempt for the noble tarragon was soon forgotten. The possibility that her eggs might find themselves cooked with the aristocratic herb sent Mrs B—— into such a state of excitement that Lady Cumberland would have risen to leave were it not for the promise of luncheon. Instead she instructed her host to produce the dish without delay: "I suggest you begin."

Mrs B—— obliged by beating the eggs slightly to break up yolks and whites. On Lady Cumberland's instruction she then passed the eggs through a sieve to remove the thread and further mix the white and yolk without creating the froth that can be "so unsightly". No sooner had such an end been reached than she added the tarragon, which was by now high in her good graces. She could barely hold back her raptures at how good the tarragon and eggs looked together and anticipated the happy moment when she would see them united, on toast.

Taking half the butter, Mrs B—— spread it around the pan, and pronounced it to be the most tractable of ingredients. The remaining butter she added in small lumps to the mixture, together with salt and pepper, before cooking the whole over a gentle heat, stirring constantly and scraping the bottom of the pan as she did so. As soon as the attachment seemed to strengthen she removed the dish from the heat and kept stirring; the warmth of the pan was sufficient to complete the cooking before the eggs became too dry.

This delightful union Mrs B—— then served with toasted bread, and with so much good taste and true merit that, when Lady Cumberland was obliged to declare the dish acceptable, the happiness of her guests was assured. And so it proved to be the case, with the possible exception of Mrs Eliot, who, when she detailed the particulars to her husband, remarked on the lack of finery or parade in the table setting and on the inferiority of the dish next to her own eggs benedict. But, in spite of all these deficiencies, the hopes, the sensitivities and the appetites of the small band of true friends who gathered for luncheon were fully answered in the perfect success of the union.

Quick Miso Soup

à la Franz Kafka

3 dessertspoons fermented miso
150g silken tofu
4–5 small mushrooms
A few leaves of dried wakame
Soy sauce

K. recognised that if a man is not always on his guard this kind of thing can happen. He was looking into the refrigerator and found it to be almost completely bare, apart from some mushrooms, which he began to slice. His guests sat waiting at the table and yet he appeared to have little to offer them. Whether he had invited them or whether they had arrived uninvited was not clear. If it were the first case he was angry with himself for failing to engage a cook for the evening so that he might command some authority at the table; for now his visitors were looking towards him as though he were a subordinate whose inefficiency was delaying their dinner. But in the second case they could hardly expect to be fed, arriving unexpectedly at such a time. The sound of a kettle boiling brought his attention back to the food and at the same time he noticed a jar of fermented miso and a block of silken tofu, perhaps left by his landlady. He placed three spoonfuls of the miso into a saucepan and poured on two pints of hot water, shielding the process from the panel as he did so. He became angry with himself for thinking of the new arrivals as a panel; they had not announced their purpose in calling on him and as yet he did not know what position each of them held. Their manner suggested, perhaps, that they were higher officials but it was also quite possible that he was their superior and they were calling on him merely to create a good impression.

With shame K. realised that he had not offered his guests anything to drink, but when he looked up he saw that a bottle was open on the table and the judges were already enjoying his wine. He found it abominable that they had served themselves without permission, but he knew their impertinence was not without significance. K. decided to shame them for their rudeness. "How is the wine?" he called. But the ruse backfired. "It would be better with some food," they chorused. "But since you have not even granted us the courtesy of dressing for dinner we do not have high hopes." K. could scarcely believe it as he noticed with discomfort that he was, indeed, in shirt and drawers.

When the soup was simmering, K. cut the tofu into one-centimetre cubes and dropped it into the steaming pan with the mushrooms and some wakame. Looking out of the window into the darkness he noticed that a girl was watching from the neighbouring house. The girl's severe expression was not unattractive to K., but the thought that she was deriving some pleasure from his situation sent him into a fury and he struck the worktop with his fist. It occurred to him that she might in some way be attached to the interrogation commission or could influence his case, and he looked beseechingly towards her, but she had backed away now and he might already have thrown away any advantages that his situation bestowed upon him. In two minutes the soup was ready. K. poured it into bowls and served his visitors. One of the four chairs around the table had been removed and, not without discomfort, K. saw that the panel was making no effort to make room for him. He added a splash of soy sauce to each of the bowls while the elder of the three judges addressed the others as if K. were invisible. "He needs to rid himself of a great many illusions; it's possible he imagines that we are subordinates calling on him to win his approval."

K.'s feeling that he was an outsider at his own dinner party was not unfamiliar. He was sorry that he was not dressed in his grey suit: its elegant cut had caused a sensation among his friends, and it was of the utmost importance to create a good impression in these situations. It was essential for a man in his position not to appear surprised by events and, as the interrogation commission divided the contents of K's bowl between them, K. stood still and tried to collect himself, for he knew that great demands would be made upon him and the soup might yet influence the outcome of his case.

Rich Chocolate Cake

à la Irvine Welsh

250g butter
500g sugar
40g cocoa
250ml coffee
150g milk chocolate
2 eggs
275g self-raising flour
375ml port

For the icing:
200g dark chocolate
100g caster sugar
100ml double cream
100ml Kahlúa (optional)

Ah make ma way back to the shithole that ah call home, wi aw the gear ah need, but ah kin barely move. Ma heid is throbbing like it's aboot tae burst, showering passers-by wi brain and bone, and ah'm so fuckin frail ma legs could snap as ah climb the stairs. Ah hope nae fucker's seen me coming back. Ah dinnae want to share any of this shite wi ma so-called friends.

Ah drop a packet of butter intae the pan and light the flame beneath it. As it melts, ah pour on the sugar, watching the white grains dissolve intae the golden brown liquid. They're dissolving cleanly; it's good fuckin shite. Ma hands are shaking as ah sprinkle the brown powder of the cocoa intae the pan and when ah drop in the bar of chocolate ah have the satisfaction of watching it melt straight away. This is a quality fuckin cook-up.

As the mixture begins to bubble and spit ah find ah'm oot of coffee, but a quick scramble under the settee produces a mug of the stuff and ah'm no fuckin goin back doon those stairs. Intae the brew it goes. The pain in ma heid is beginning to subside and, what wi the smell of the gear cookin and the calming sight of the gas flame, ah'm feeling better already.

Ah take the pan off the heat while ah crack two eggs into a jug. Ma eyes focus long enough oan the shells tae read the crack-by date: the bastards want me tae throw them oot and buy more. Mebbe the hen that laid them is sitting in the freezer doon at Scotmid, but ah know they keep for months. There's nae need tae beat the eggs: the 14.22 from King's Cross goes by the windae and stirs every fuckin thing, including me. Ah measure oot the flour and at the sight of such a mountain of white powder ah'm tempted tae stick ma nose in. Ah add the eggs and flour to the mixture and pour oan a drop of port. Ah hae a drop masel; it's no bad, so ah put some more intae the pan. The bottle's soon finished. Ah've drunk half and the other half's goan intae the mixture – greedy fuckin cake.

There's a knock at the door. Fuck. Ah ignore it. Ma heid is beginning tae throb again and ah decide it's time tae hit the bevvies. Ah've enough cans of special tae see me through till the cookin's over, if nae fucker comes in. The knocking starts again, only this time it's louder.

– Stevie, ah know yer in there, open the fucking door.

It's Spanner, ma so-called best mate. No way am ah sharing any of this gear wi him, but he's gaunnae take the door off the hinges. Ah open up.

– Moan in Span, it's guid tae see yer. Can you spot me a twenty til ma giro arrives in the mornin.

It nearly fucking works. He's aboot tae turn round, but his nose must still contain some traces of functionality, because he starts sniffin the air like a dug.

– Yer cookin up, Stevie. Ah kin tell.

He goes straight in tae the kitchen and by the time ah've closed the door he's opened one of ma cans and is holding his heid over the pan, breathing deeply. What kin ye do?

There's a mountain of the brown stuff in the pan, so ah grease two cake tins and pour the mixture in. Ah can hardly wait. Ah'm tempted to eat it as it is, but the last thing ah need is a fuckin bad chocolate trip. The tins go intae the oven at 200 degrees. Ah cook everything at the same temperature; ah fuckin hate those yuppie bastards with their fan-assisted bollocks and temperatures. When you're cookin, you're cookin, end ay fuckin story.

– How long Stevie?

Spanner's as desperate as ah am.

– Aboot an hour.

– Kin it be quicker?

– Ah'm cookin as fast as ah can and yer nae fuckin help.

Spanner's aboot as much use in the kitchen as an amputated prick at a hoor's convention, an ah can tell he's been oan the bevvies. While he's away for a pish, ah put the dark chocolate in a pan and measure oot the caster sugar. Ah add the cream and Kahlúa tae the pan. Kahlúa's a fuckin lassie's drink, ah know, but it's no bad in a cake. When ah go tae the scales for the sugar Spanner's already there, aboot tae start shovelling the white powder up his hooter. I dinnae shout stop, but the penny soon drops. He's greetin like hell as he sticks his nose under the tap, while ah'm stirring the sugar into the pan.

Ah kin hear someone calling ma name. For a moment ah think it's a voice in ma heid, calling me back to planet earth, but ah soon catch on. It's another fucking unwelcome visitor. They'll go soon enough; but Spanner, ever useless, opens the windae and shouts down. Hiddy and Gav are standing in the street, suited and booted. They both work for Grenson's the undertakers, and the two cunts have come around in the company car. Ah owe Gav a fifty and he's no one tae forget. What does he expect? Gav and Hiddy are the only poor fuckers tae get a job, since the social caught em signing on fer five different addresses. They'll no be riding the giro d'écosse for a while.

– Stevie's cooking up.

Ah'm tempted tae lift Span's feet and tip him oot the windae, the big-mouthed cunt, but ah dinnae have the strength. Gav and Hiddy are soon at the door with what sounds like a battering ram. Spanner lets them in, while ah grab another can of heavy before those greedy bastards drink the lot. Gav staggers in looking the man, in a black suit and tie.

– How long Stevie? We've got tae nash.

Hiddy is behind him and between them they're carrying a fuckin coffin.

–Sorry Stevie, the last time we left the car it wis stolen. We got the car back but the body wis missing. It's the sack if we lose another.

Hiddy kin barely breathe. The effort of climbing the stairs has nearly finished him off. They dump the box on the floor and Hiddy collapses into a chair, the skin on his face stretched like cling film over his skull. He could swap places with the man in the box and you'd no notice the difference. Ah go to close the door and see a wee lassie standing in the hall. She's wearing a black coat five sizes too big and her face is as white as a sheet. Ah look at Gav.

–Aw Stevie, this is Debbie. That's her boyfriend in the box. We'll no be long, Debbie, moan in.

She has the look of one of those lassies whae'll do anything tae please. She isn't makin any fuss aboot her boyfriend's little detour on his way to his last resting place, that's fer sure. She sits oan the settee hugging hersel. She's nae bad, she won't be oan her puff for long. Ah'll fuckin move in there, pretty sharpish an aw. Then ah notice she's nae hugging hersel; she's holding a bairn under that big coat. It starts greetin and she gets oot one of her tits tae feed it. The cheeky slut's only breast-feeding, in ma hoose. Ah what the fuck, ah've got tae finish the icing. Gav and Hiddy hae forgotten their hurry and are hittin the bevvies, their feet up on Debbie's boyfriend's wooden overcoat. If it fits him like Debbie's coat fits her, the poor bastard must've been a midget.

The hour is nearly up. Ah warm through the icing and

remove the cake tins from the cooker. Ah find a syringe and needle, ideal for checking the middle of the cake is cooked. Nae problem, the needle is clean. Oan the outside the cake is burnt, so ah cut off the burnt bits and slap on the icing while it's still hot. The two slabs sit there glistening, like bars of brown bullion. Spanner has by now drunk the rest of the Kahlúa, and is oot of his box, jumping around desperate for a piece of the brown stuff. He can fuckin wait. Ah'm feeling sorry for the wee lassie so she'll come first – after me, of course. The crowd are all smiles as ah come into the room wi a big plate of chocolate salvation, and Debbie's boyfriend makes a nice wee coffee table.

We're all soon stuffing our faces, though ah would'nae recommend the heavy as the ideal accompaniment. Wee Debbie is getting in the swing. She's put the bairn oan the floor wi a piece of cake to stop his greeting and she's cramming a piece of the dark slice intae her gob, her eyes rolling back in her head, like if she eats enough chocolate it'll stop all the pain. Spanner, as usual, has overdone it. The Kahlúa does nae mix well with the heavy, the cake and whativir he had before he arrived. He's back at the windae; who the fuck is arriving now? But he's no talking; he's spewing intae the street, lazy fuck. Spanner is the original come-back kid, and two minutes later he picks up the last piece of cake.

– It's no bad – he says – But it's no the same as skag.

No bad? The fucker's eaten huf of it.

Gav and Hiddy are back on their feet, struggling tae pick up their quiet friend.

– Thanks Stevie, we've got tae nash, says Gav – Don't forget that fifty you owe us.

Rich Chocolate Cake

Ah'm just in time to remove a plate from the coffee table before it's repossessed, and they're away. But ah've goat Debbie's address. Ah look oot the windae: down below they make a pretty wee procession, all in black, weaving from side to side, like Archie Gemmill in slow motion. But the car's no looking too good. Spanner's scored a direct hit. It looks like some fucker's tried tae give the car a chocolate icing, but Gav and Hiddy dinnae notice and they're soon loaded up and off. What kin ye do? He's no the first person tae be carried in and oot of ma place. Nor is he the first to drive off covered with vomit. But credit tae him, he's brought something new tae the game, the poor bastard. Don't get me wrong, ah dinnae feel sorry for him, ah'll be following in his footsteps soon enough. Ah'm the one ah feel sorry fer. What am ah doing that's so fuckin new? We think we're the centre of the universe, but we're not. What's the universe anyway? It's just a great big fuckin roundaboot that we're all going round endlessly and there's nothing we kin do aboot it. We live we die. End of fuckin story.

Tiramisu

à la Marcel Proust

12–15 Savoiardi sponge fingers
4 eggs
100g caster sugar
Amaretto di Saronno
500g mascarpone
2 cups cold coffee
Cocoa powder

Although the fashionableness of any café and its degree of comfort usually stand in inverse relation to each other, on a cold day in March I found myself on the Boulevard Beaumarchais, in a café, whose owners, from their headquarters no doubt far from the district in which I now sat, had succeeded in finding the precise median such that the establishment offered neither style nor comfort; its combination of brown sofas, blonde wood and red walls looked like it had been delivered in a single packing case, from a world which knew nothing of the one to which it was expediting its wares, the result being a mediocrity so well researched that it shouted its presence. Looking now at the cappuccino served to me in the crude white mug, the surface of which had been whipped into a frenzy of froth and too liberally sprinkled with chocolate, I lamented the fact that my age now required me to stop and rest when my body demanded it and not when my eyes were attracted by something or someone too tempting to resist. Yet when I sipped at the beverage, suddenly the memory appeared; the chocolate powder sprinkled on my cappuccino became the cocoa on the surface of the tiramisu that I had first tasted one evening in the garden at Combray, where my father was holding a small party to welcome the former ambassador to Rome, who had recently returned to the neighbourhood with his daughter.

From this ancient past – its great houses gone and its inhabitants dwindling, like the last creatures of a mythical forest – came something infinitely more frail and yet more alive, insubstantial yet persistent; the memories of smell and taste, so faithful, resisted the destruction and rebuilt for a moment the palace wherein dwelt the remembrance of that evening and of that tiramisu.

The combination of cream and coffee seemed to offer access to a world more real than that in which I sat, this pretender that announced itself the 'home of coffee', whose distinct signage of 'Simply Delicious', 'Come in for Lunch', 'Hot Panini' called to a generation to whom I was lost. Did any of its clientele know of the beauty of the Café Florian on St Mark's Square where my ancestors had once taken coffee with Byron? The memory gone, I sipped again at the hot beverage; once more the recollection came of that first experience, the evening at Combray when I was introduced to Ursula Patrignani, her body flexing like a prima ballerina, bowing in a show of mock courtesy as she handed me a small bowl of tiramisu, and of the slight dizziness I felt in her presence as I looked at the movement of her exquisite Botticelli mouth, too dazed to hear her words. The very unsteadiness of my legs became the rocking of a gondola, as we docked at a Venetian Palazzo and walked arm in arm through the mist into a room graced by Bellini's *Feast of the Gods*. Again the memory faded, and the decaying eau-de-nil walls of the palazzo and the works of the Venetian masters were replaced by red and brown panels and over-enlarged photographs depicting young people in casual dress drinking coffee. I feared that the recipe was lost to me forever.

The creamy draught had cooled; its flavour seemed to be dying already and with it remembrance of that evening. Sensing that the memories had not departed forever and were lingering like souls after death, I ordered a second cup of the milky drink which might in other circumstances have disgusted me; now I craved it as if it were the elixir of youth and capable of curing my old age. "The same, Monsieur?" asked the young waitress. "I am sorry but before I gave you one flavoured with almond syrup by mistake." The poor girl looked anxious, but I nearly kissed those delicate white hands of hers from gratitude; it was the sweet almond taste that had awoken that beauty from its sleep in the dark forest of past memory, recalling the Amaretto di Saronno that I had tasted for the first time that night with Ursula Patrignani in the gaslight among the chrysanthemums. The waitress smiled as she served what was for her just another drink, but for me the liquid was a hallucinatory potion that could open the doors of

21

my perception; her consciousness had barely registered my presence because I was only partly in her world, choosing to probe this portal to truths which dwelt in a realm more real than hers.

This time I closed my eyes and sipped deeply of the draught, realising that what I sought dwelt not in the cappuccino but within myself. This white-hooded potion was my guide down to the underworld, and would assist in shaking free the anchor that kept these elusive memories so firmly held in the depths of my consciousness.

Separate from the others we now talked; hidden by the chrysanthemums, and knowing that no one could see how foolish I must look, I gathered my courage, resolving to ask her to marry me there and then, but as I opened my mouth to speak she gently fed to me a teaspoonful of the delightful mixture, and I was silenced. Never before had I accepted to take food in such a way except from my mother as she gave me my medicine before kissing me goodnight. As I swallowed the heavenly concoction I found myself imbued with an unknown courage; I had to make her understand what I was feeling. "I am experiencing something that I have never felt before," I told her, but before I could continue, she spoke. "I know, it happens to everyone the first time. Chef's tiramisu is simply sublime; Father says that it has saved us from a thousand international incidents and that without it he could never have maintained a peaceful Europe. Madame Verdurin has tried everything to get the recipe, but Father wouldn't give it even to the Duke of Milan." My feelings for her were so intense that I grew light-headed, confused my thoughts with my speech and became unsure of what I had said out loud or thought to myself. Did she feel anything for me? Could she find it in her heart to reciprocate the profound feelings that I had for her? Involuntarily I cried out, "I must know." Whether she really misunderstood me or coquettishly chose to interpret my question in such a way as to keep alive the tantalising doubt that made my mind so feverish, she continued, "You shall know. Chef begins always with the coffee, fresh and strong, but chilled in ice, so that it doesn't dissolve the Savoiardi, the little sponge fingers that are sent regularly from Italy. These he dips into the coffee, turning them, before laying them in the bowl to form the foundation for his creation. The secret is that he always laces the coffee with the amaretto, which he keeps at hand throughout the process." I could barely remain on my feet. "He then takes the eggs and separates out the yolks, which he mixes with sugar to form a soft cream. The whites he whisks into a snowy peak." To throw myself from that snow-swept mountain. "He then reunites the two mixtures," o blessed union, "before adding the mascarpone a little at a time and a final splash of the amaretto. He then spreads the creamy concoction on top of the sponge fingers and continues with alternating layers until the last layer of cream, which he covers with cocoa powder shaken from the sieve, taking care not to miss an inch." At this I staggered backwards and fainted.

When I recovered consciousness I was in my bed at Combray, my mother touching my shoulder to wake me. At the touch of her hand I looked up. "I'm sorry, Monsieur, but would you mind moving to a smaller table?" A group of young mothers with perambulators waited in the doorway, looking towards me. My cup sat empty on the table and I walked out onto the busy Parisian boulevard.

Coq au Vin

à la Gabriel García Márquez

1 whole chicken, c. 3½ kg
800g baby onions
200g smoked pork
2 carrots
5 cloves of garlic
3 sticks of celery
3 leeks
A few leaves of sage
Olive oil

Marinade:
2 medium onions
1 sprig of rosemary
1 small bunch of thyme
3 cloves
Coriander and mustard seeds
Juniper berries
Red peppercorns
1 litre red wine

Father Antonio del Sacramento del Altar Castañeda sat in the garden and watched the afternoon die. The darkness had begun to grow as heavy as the heat, and he held off going into the inferno of the house as long as he could. But he had smoked his last cigar and was now unarmed as the mosquitoes enveloped him, and he was forced to retreat into the gaslit interior.

The light of the kitchen dazzled him as he closed the door on the swarm. He slapped his neck, killing a winged intruder before it could feast, and reflected on the last rites. Earlier that day he had visited the murderer Fidel Agosto Santiago to hear his confession, but the prisoner had declared himself unready. Santiago would eat his last supper the following night, and since the condemned man refused to accept food from his wife, the priest had taken on the responsibility. He sprayed the room with insecticide and began to cough.

Guiltily he looked across at Tobaga, the haughty mulatta who had prepared his evening meal every night for the last fifteen years. Watching her in the kitchen was a pleasure he had denied himself in his more venereal years, but that appetite was now a faint glow whose embers' warmth would only be extinguished by any attempt to refuel them. As she washed her hands he felt the need to urinate and left the room. His once powerful flow, which had reverberated in the night bucket with the sound of a stallion galloping, was reduced to a trickle, the intense ammonia smell of which rivalled the fumes that drifted in at dusk from the swamp and filled him with the sadness of decay.

When he returned to the kitchen Tobaga was preparing the marinade that would bathe the cockerel, that toughest of birds, for two days. "It is for Fidel. The Syrian's servant came today with the cockerel." The priest sat down and thought of the task that awaited him at the prison, but was startled from his thoughts by the sound of Tobaga chopping the bird into pieces. Each time she brought the cleaver down her dress swayed and the contours of her body made themselves more visible. She dropped the head into a bucket and Father Antonio felt a sharp prick on his neck, before bringing his hand down and killing the last survivor of the earlier siege.

Tobaga sliced two onions and added them to the cockerel in the pot. She covered the pieces with wine and, as they bathed in the blood-red liquid, she added juniper berries, coriander, mustard and red peppercorns, cloves and, finally, the rosemary and thyme. She then left the pot to marinate in the marble-lined pantry, the only cool place in the house, and one to which Father Antonio would retreat on afternoons of calamitous heat.

"When will the food be ready?" he asked.

"The marinade must be allowed to work for forty-eight hours," answered Tobaga.

"Can it be shorter?"

She looked at him, her eyes like golden almonds. "For a bird such as this?" And he knew it could not. The cockerel was a gift from the Syrian. Known as El Jaguarcito, The Little Jaguar, it had been the most successful of all his fighting birds. It had earned the Syrian a small fortune and its sacrifice was a mark of the debt he felt towards the condemned man. The priest turned a blind eye to the gambling and bloodshed of the cockfights but knew enough of El Jaguarcito's reputation to understand. "I will speak to the mayor in the morning."

Father Antonio rose, as he always did, at five, and dressed in darkness. Outside dawn struggled to rouse itself as he walked the short distance to the church. The carnivorous cloud had descended once again and he raised the hood of his cassock until he was safely within the nave. As the worshippers arrived, each brought with them their own grief, an emptiness that dwarfed the nave. The insomniac was already there; it was rumoured that he had not slept for 75 years, except during Mass. The second to arrive was a woman who had recently lost her second son; like the first, he had been bitten by a rabid dog, but before the disease had been able to reach its violent zenith she had poisoned him. The last to arrive was the wife of the condemned man. The priest spoke without conviction and the Mass was brief. When the chance to leave came, pausing to remove a cockroach from the font, he headed in the direction of the mayor's house.

Like a marionette, whose strings might break at any moment, the town was stirring. A pair of black macaws flew overhead and the priest quickened his pace. A boy emerged from a temporary shelter at the side of the river and howled at the moon; he laughed at his joke and the priest shivered. Further on he overtook a family that appeared to be pushing all its belongings in a cart. A little girl led the way marching solemnly as she carried a vase of black peonies, and a boy at the rear of the family group held a cage which contained a white dove.

The mayor was half-dressed and sat with his braces over his bare shoulders. His wife did not greet the priest but silently poured coffee for the two men, looking on with her black-ringed eyes. "Thank God," said the mayor. "Another two hours before we start sweating again."

"I need a stay of execution," the priest said, without looking up from his coffee.

"Impossible. The soldiers are already on their way. They will arrive tomorrow."

"He has requested coq au vin and it will take two days to prepare."

"So it's true that the Syrian slaughtered El Jaguarcito?"

"El Jaguarcito is sitting in a pot in my kitchen."

The mayor crossed himself. "Can it not be cooked today?"

"Tobaga says it will be a crime before heaven. We cannot give Fidel Agosto Santiago a half-cooked last supper."

The mayor had no wish to disappoint Father Antonio or the condemned man, who had at one time been the greatest chef in the area. He sipped at his coffee and walked out onto the balcony. "If I agree, it will be to honour the Little Jaguar, not from sympathy for Fidel Santiago." Father Antonio knew that he had succeeded.

"Will you be at Mass on Sunday?" the priest asked as he was leaving.

"Say a prayer for me, Father."

A troupial was singing as the priest headed for the prison. Fidel Santiago sat gambling with his guards. One of the soldiers had lost his horse to the prisoner. The prison house was full of tobacco smoke and the priest coughed. When Father Antonio gave Fidel the news, the condemned man let out a deep sigh. "Tell her not to forget the sage, Father, just a few leaves."

The men returned to their gambling and the priest went out into the growing heat.

On the eve of the execution Father Antonio took up his

position at the kitchen table and laid out the church accounts. Tobaga crossed herself, took the pieces of the Little Jaguar from the marinade and allowed them to drain. In a pan she heated the olive oil and added the small onions, whole. She chopped the smoked pork into small pieces and put that, too, into the pan. Into this last arena, slowly and with great circumspection, she now laid the pieces of the Little Jaguar. The body parts spat furiously as they touched the burning oil. When the flesh had turned golden Tobaga covered the carnage with the blood-red marinade and El Jaguarcito was silenced forever. She cut the carrots finely, her breasts making a little jump each time the blade struck the chopping board. The garlic cloves she left en chemise, their paper-dry covers like the sleeping pupae of butterflies that will never emerge. These she threw into the mixture, before adding the celery, leeks and seasoning. She covered the pan; the flames probed inquisitively at its base as she left it on a medium heat for an hour or so. His accounts untouched, Father Antonio closed his eyes and slipped into a siesta while Tobaga kept the vigil, never allowing the pan to run dry, constantly adding liquid from the marinade.

When the time came, Tobaga lifted the pieces of El Jaguarcito from the sauce. As she did so Father Antonio woke with a start. "Sleep on. I will wake you when it's ready," said Tobaga.

"I was dreaming that the food was poisoned and that the firing squad, refusing to be cheated, took me in his place."

"They may yet come for you."

Tobaga passed the sauce through a sieve, then, after touching the liquid and sucking on her finger, added more salt and continued to heat it. When she found the consistency she was seeking she returned the pieces of the cockerel to the liquid and added the sage leaves. A quarter of an hour later she woke the priest with a look. "The cockerel is ready," she said, and she saw the fear in his movements as he rose. "I can take the food to him, if you wish," she added.

"You can go later, but I will hear his confession first. He will not eat until his conscience is clear." And Father Antonio took up the dish and went out into the heat of the evening. As Tobaga watched him go she saw the carnivorous cloud descend to accompany him; the mosquitoes would feed as far as the prison.

Mushroom Risotto

à la John Steinbeck

Extra virgin olive oil
25g porcini mushrooms
3 field mushrooms
1 onion
2 cloves garlic
200g risotto rice
500ml vegetable stock
Salt and pepper
60g Parmesan
1 glass white wine

The porcini lay dry and wrinkled, each slice twisted by thirst and the colour of parched earth. When the water finally fell, at first only in splashes, they drank what they could, but soon they were all covered with the life-giving liquid. The parched fragments recovered an earlier form, their contortions changed, by the gift of water, into a supine mass, glistening. What had resembled a bowl of tree bark now had the rich colour of cooked meat, the purple brown of wet soil had replaced the dry plaster of Arizona earth. The cook left them like this to soak for 45 minutes.

The first oil, extra virgin, poured into the heavy-bottomed pan, and as the flame licked at the metal, it grew more liquid. The field mushrooms were cool to the touch. Their thin skin and soft white bodies yielded to the knife and the slices piled up on the chopping board. The cook wrinkled her nose as she caught the scent of hot oil and lowered the heat before frying the mushrooms. Their pale flesh soaked up the green liquid, and as the heat surged up through the pan, they turned brown and golden, their once perfect matt surface now shining with an oily sheen.

The heat was now everywhere and irresistible. The fire flared up, steady and unbroken; without a flicker the flame worked at the underside of the pan. The cook wiped her brow with her hand as she turned the mushrooms, browning in the pan. Once ready they were put to one side. Fresh oil was added. The porcini were poured into a sieve; their liquid, dark and brackish, she collected to be used later. Nothing was wasted. The drained porcini slid sizzling into the hot oil, which struggled with the water in their flesh. With a cover the cook muffled the voice of the porcini. The steam condensed on the underside of the lid and dripped back into the pan, recreating the cycle of the rains.

Her scarred and calloused hands peeled the onion and garlic before chopping them finely. She knew the porcini would make it if the pan didn't dry out; the moisture would be needed for the work ahead. When ready, the porcini, too, were set aside and the onion and garlic took their place. Their scent rose like a cloud and the cook stood back, her eyes smarting. The onion grew transparent and soft and gave of its juices. She covered the vegetables with a lid. They murmured and whimpered until they turned to a soft juicy pap. Then the rice rained down onto the onion and garlic, each drop glistening as it was turned in the oil. A drought rain taking moisture where it fell, the rice began to soak up the liquid. As it was added, the porcini stock made a rushing, bubbling sound, like waves breaking at Pebble Beach, and the white grains began to swell, slowly. Soon the liquid was gone. Seasoning was added, and now the vegetable stock was needed, a little at a time, like the movement of the seasons.

The Parmesan cheese was hard and dry. The cook grated what little she had. The cheese grated coarsely, like maize from the thresher; the cheese grated finely, like the first powder snow; the cheese grated in shavings, like the wood thrown up from her husband's plane. She divided the Parmesan and mixed half into the nearly cooked rice, along with the mushrooms and porcini. The mixture grew thick, and she poured on a shot of white wine before giving a final stir.

She shared the mixture out carefully in the cracked bowls, and sprinkled on the last of the Parmesan. It wasn't meat and potatoes, but at least her family would eat tonight.

Boned stuffed poussins

à la Marquis de Sade

2 poussins
85g butter
1 large onion
110g button mushrooms, sliced
55g fresh white breadcrumbs
2 tablespoons fresh parsley, finely chopped
Grated rind of a quarter of a lemon
30g prunes, soaked overnight
30g dried apricots, soaked overnight
Salt and freshly ground black pepper
Half a beaten egg
170g mixed chopped onion, carrot, turnip and celery
290ml chicken stock
1 bay leaf
Watercress to garnish

Should not the supreme aim of gastronomy be to untangle the
confusion of ideas that confront mankind, and to provide this
unfortunate biped with some guidance as to how he should

conduct himself and his appetites? Buffeted continually by the studies of scientists, the inventions of dieticians, the fashions of restaurateurs and the disguised marketing campaigns of a thousand trade associations, his own tastes are often his last point of reference. The tyranny of political correctness, undermining him further, makes of him a man who avoids endangered species, factory farming, deforestation, genetic modification and inhumane slaughter. If he is unfortunate enough also to have a religion, then he will probably live the meanest of lives in the most tightly fitting of gastronomic straitjackets. By walking such a culinary tightrope, he believes that he will reap his rewards in long life, good health, moral superiority and in heaven hereafter. Yet all around him our unfortunate sees good vegetarians pushing up daisies, teetotallers' hearts tightening and sugarphobes queueing in dentists' waiting rooms. Reader, recognise that all your years of abstinence and your naive trust in low-fat yoghurt have not saved you from a pot belly, heavy jowls and an inadequate sex drive. A life of dieting has rendered your face pinched and furrowed from harsh judgement of your fellow diners and your evenings long and lonely.

Not all of our revered chefs eat the food that they recommend so strongly to us and there are many whose appetites are best expressed behind closed doors. It is with these observations in mind that we take up our pen, and in consideration of their wisdom we ask of you, reader, your full attention for this recipe which I recommend to you, told to me by an innocent girl, Justine, who recently had the good fortune to come under my tutelage.

Judge Hugon was one of these high priests of abstinence,

and his table was noted for its correctness. Dressed only in black and white, his visits to the local church struck fear into the preacher, who felt the eye of the judge upon him as if the Almighty himself were standing in judgement. The judge was noted for his rectitude in all matters and his home, frequented by lawyers and politicians, was a fortress of political correction. The judge had taken a vow of abstinence from all unworthy food: endangered cod, non-line-caught tuna, prawns farmed amid the destruction of mangrove swamps and the meat of all living creatures possessed of a soul. Finally, the further to set him apart from his fellow men, his wife, once in possession of three fine children, had invited him to sleep in the guest room.

One afternoon a knock at the door disturbed the judge from his correspondence. He found on the doorstep a timid-looking girl, her delicate countenance a picture of modesty. Her virginal air and large blue eyes, clear complexion, bright white teeth and beautiful blonde hair demonstrated a candour and good faith that were sure to lead her into trouble. This charming young girl was, in fact, the daughter of the local butcher and, when her father's deliveryman had been taken ill at work, in good faith she had offered her services. Unfamiliar with the poor script of her father's employee, she had misread an address and now found herself, not at number 27 The Avenue, home of a well-known bon viveur, but instead delivering two fine poussins to number 21, residence of a man who had renounced all pleasures involving flesh. This is her tale as she told it to me:

"The house was grand and at the end of a long drive bordered on both sides by a high hedge. The black door looked so grand, in fact, that I was quite in awe and, knowing that I was very late with the deliveries, due to my misfortune in the residents' parking area, I was little prepared for the stern figure who opened the door to me. 'Oh sir, I am sorry to be so late with your poussins. My van was clamped and I have had to finish the last of the deliveries on foot.' I must have looked exhausted from my exertions and my voice seemed to touch a chord in the judge. 'Sweet child, I forgive you,' he said breathlessly. 'Won't you come in and drink something?' Looking left and right, he took the package from me and showed me into a long hall. It was not cold in the house but I noticed that he was trembling as he closed the door. 'I'm sure we can deal with the clamp on your van.' The judge made me answer a number of questions, while he listened with an air of great piety. 1. Was his house definitely the last delivery of the day? 2. Was it true that I was not expected back promptly at my father's shop? 3. Was I sure that once the deliveries were over I was to take the day off? 4. Had I parked the van well away from the house?

"When I had fully satisfied him on these points he seemed to relax. 'There, there, my child, so you won't be missed for a while, and we have plenty of time to deal with these birds, I mean, deal with your stranded vehicle. Let me make a quick telephone call; my office has few benefits, but I am, I hope, not without some power in dealing with your current predicament.'

"He was a very large man, closely shaved with pale skin and piercing grey eyes, and for some reason I was beginning to regret accepting his help. 'I have troubled you enough already, sir; I will walk back to the shop and tell my father.'

This seemed to make him angry: 'Are you afraid of a member of Her Majesty's bench? Do you doubt that I would act in any way but that which is most just? How dare you.' With that, he grasped my wrist and shoved me into what appeared to be the pantry. I heard the door being locked from outside and found myself alone in the dark. I banged on the door shouting for help but when there was no response I gave up my cries. As my eyes adjusted to the darkness I could see I was in a small store-room, lined with shelves on which stood well-ordered packages of wholewheat pasta, boxes of GMO-free oats, packets of rice crackers and jars of sugar-free jam. Noticing the keyhole, I bent down to look through. The sight that met my eyes left me trembling. 'O holy father, am I to be the victim of my good nature and daughterly devotion?'

"Outside, the judge was slowly peeling away the wrapping to reveal two fleshy white birds, breasts uppermost. I saw his eyes widen and he began talking to the two poussins. 'What have we here? Two naughty little birds.' As he spoke he gave one of them a playful slap. 'We will need to teach you a lesson.' Placing a hand on each bird he gave them a squeeze. 'You have nothing to fear, my little chicks; it is I who am corrupted. Whilst I will break my vow before heaven and must expect the harshest judgement, your innocent souls perch in paradise.'

"He then began to bone the poussins with a kitchen knife. I'm sure my father must have done this on many occasions but I had never watched before. The judge was labouring over the task and sweat dripped from his forehead onto the plump white birds. The job took him some time and he strained and grunted as he worked, using such language that you will forgive me if

I refrain from reporting every word of his frightful discourse. Reaching a pause he looked up from his work towards the pantry from which I witnessed his abuses while trembling for my own safety, and he appeared to address the poussins: 'Now, my chicks, you have been well and truly boned. But there is so much more that we can do; how about a little stuffing?' And he took a packet of butter and placed a lump into a pan to melt over a low heat while the villain chopped a large onion. He proceeded to cook the onion gently and then added some sliced button mushrooms. As I watched him, now chopping a bunch of parsley, the odour of the food began to drift in through the keyhole and as my appetite reminded me that I had not eaten since breakfast, I momentarily forgot my predicament.

"I was soon reminded of my situation when my captor began muttering to himself. Although I could not hear him clearly I caught the words 'fresh, white, succulent fruit', and nearly fainted with fear when I saw him walking towards my prison door. I covered my eyes and instinctively cowered on the floor. The door opened and I felt his footsteps as he entered the pantry. Then I heard the clink of glass, and the door slammed shut again as he left. Had my sobs roused some mercy in this monster? I looked through the keyhole, expecting to see him doubting his vile course of action, but was instead greeted by the sight of him arranging three jars on the worktop: prunes, dried apricots and breadcrumbs. He added the breadcrumbs and a good handful of the chopped parsley to the onion mixture, before grating some lemon rind on top and stirring in the chopped dried fruits. He added salt and pepper and, finally, the beaten egg.

"All the time the judge's eyes seemed crazed by a deep

hunger that had cast aside his judgement leaving only a deter-
mination to satisfy his bodily appetites without check or
hindrance; I trembled as I witnessed this eruption. The white
shirt that had seemed so well laundered was now splattered
with blood and butter stains. I watched, horrified, as he licked
the beaten egg from his fingers and then wiped them down his
shirt. If he had answered the door in such a state he could
never have taken advantage of my naivety. He now laid the
two poussins down in front of him and began to stuff them
with the mixture. I had no idea that a small bird could take so
much stuffing, but he carried on, using language that my ears
could barely suffer, until the poor birds could take no more.
Then he took a needle and thread, sewed up their openings and
patted the brutalised creatures back into shape. He dropped
another knob of butter into a large flameproof dish, and as it
foamed with the heat, browned the poussins lightly all over.
Meanwhile, the villain had chopped some winter vegetables –
onion, turnip, carrot and celery – and these he exchanged in
the pan for the now golden poussins, and added a little more
butter. I could not see clearly but believe that once the vegetables were lightly browned he placed the poussins back into
the pan and added some chicken stock. I was horrified to see
him do this using a stock cube; if the old scoundrel had not
been in such a hurry he could have made a bouillon using the
chicken bones. He added a bay leaf and seasoning and then
covered the pan and allowed it to simmer for three quarters of
an hour. I must have fainted, for, when I next opened my eyes,
the cooked poussins were being placed in the oven to keep
warm, and Judge Hugon was passing the vegetables through
a sieve to extract their juice. He discarded what was left of the

crushed vegetables and continued boiling the liquid. I gathered from his study of the spoon that he was waiting for it to take on a honey consistency.

"I feared that once this miserable creature had satisfied the most pressing of his desires it would not be long before this excess of debauchery would overflow and I should become the dish that would feed his baser appetites. I saw that a small ventilation panel high in the pantry might be forced open if I could reach it and disguise the noise of my escape. Climbing up the shelves, I began screaming to be let out and throwing boxes of low-sodium salt and soya milk to the ground. As I suspected, my abductor remained engrossed in his stuffed birds and cared not a whit. At the same time I began striking at the ventilation panel using a tin of vegetarian pâté. At last the mesh gave way; as the light flooded in I could see below me on the pantry floor a pool of white liquid made up of soya milk and rice drinks running under the door. Wasting no time I squeezed my shoulders through the gap and wriggled my legs through behind me. I found myself in the space between two houses. From fear and relief, I could barely stand; I headed for the neighbour's house, on the door of which a small plaque read 'Sir Michael Mead, MP'; here, surely, was somebody of authority who could help a poor maiden in distress and would see that the judge got his just desserts. I rang the doorbell and fainted."

You may well imagine the politician's distress on finding this poor creature on his doorstep, her clothes stained and her pulse weak. As Justine recovered her senses on his couch, the member of parliament comforted the unfortunate girl as she watered the fine fabric of his soft furnishings with her tears, until they had run their course and she was able to recount the unspeakable happenings of that day. As she spoke, the kindly man took pains to remove all trace of her suffering: the most delicate morsels were served to restore her strength, and while her clothes were taken to be washed, he arranged for the release of her father's delivery vehicle. By the time that Justine left the residence of the honourable member, assured that the accusations against Judge Hugon would be more successfully pursued by a man of influence such as himself, she felt sure in the knowledge that she had found a protector, a man of power with a good heart and respect for those weaker than himself.

No scandal followed, nor was the judge's reputation damaged in any way. Shortly after these events he was appointed Master of the Rolls, and his neighbour, the honourable member, was made a government minister. The two men were both influential at a local level and offered their support to a successful supermarket chain seeking to open a large branch in the elegant neighbourhood. Within a short time Justine's father's shop had failed, and with it his health. His devoted daughter was obliged to take on evening work in a fried chicken take-away establishment. And so it was that I had the good fortune to discover her there, late one night.

You, who have shed a tear for the misfortune of one so virtuous, you, who pity the unfortunate Justine, take comfort. If, through forces that it is not given us to understand, God allows her to be persecuted on earth, it is in order to compensate her all the more in heaven hereafter.

Clafoutis Grandmère

à la Virginia Woolf

500g cherries
3 eggs
150g flour
150g sugar
10g yeast, prepared in warm water if necessary
100g butter
1 cup of milk

She placed the cherries in a buttered dish and looked out of the window. The children were racing across the lawn, Nicholas already between the clumps of red-hot pokers, turning to wait for the others. Looking back at the cherries, that would not be pitted, red polka dots on white, so bright and jolly, their little core of hardness invisible, in pity she thought of Mrs Sorley, that poor woman with no husband and so many mouths to feed, Mrs Sorley who knew the hard core but not the softness; and she placed the dish of cherries to one side.

Gently she melted the butter, transparent and smooth,

oleaginous and clear, clarified and golden, and mixed it with the sugar in a large bowl. Should she have made something traditionally English? (Involuntarily, piles of cake rose before her eyes.) Of course the recipe was French, from her grandmother. English cooking was an abomination: it was boiling cabbages in water until they were liquid; it was roasting meat until it was shrivelled; it was cutting out the flavours with a blunt knife.

She added an egg, pausing to look up at the jacmanna, its colour so vivid against the whitewashed wall. Would it not be wonderful if Nicholas became a great artist, all life stretching before him, a blank canvas, bright coloured shapes gradually becoming clearer? There would be lovers, triumphs, the colours darkening, work, loneliness, struggle. She wished he could stay as he was now, they were so happy; the sky was so clear, they would never be as happy again. With great serenity she added an egg, for was she not descended from that very noble, French house whose female progeny brought their arts and energy, their sense of colour and shape, wit and poise to the sluggish English? She added an egg, whose yellow sphere, falling into the domed bowl, broke and poured, like Vesuvius erupting into the mixture, like the sun setting into a butter sea. Its broken shell left two uneven domes on the counter, and all the poverty and all the suffering of Mrs Sorley had turned to that, she thought.

When the flour came it was a delight, a touch left on her cheek as she brushed aside a wisp of hair, as if her beauty bored her and she wanted to be like other people, insignificant, sitting in a widow's house with her pen and paper, writing notes, understanding the poverty, revealing the social problem

(she folded the flour into the mixture). She was so command-
ing (not tyrannical, not domineering; she should not have
minded what people said), she was like an arrow set on a target.
She would have liked to build a hospital, but how? For now,
this clafoutis for Mrs Sorley and her children (she added the
yeast, prepared in warm water). The yeast would cause the
mixture to rise up into the air like a column of energy, nurtured
by the heat of the oven, until the arid kitchen knife of the male,
cutting mercilessly, plunged itself into the dome, leaving it flat
and exhausted.

Little by little she added the milk, stopping only when the
mixture was fluid and even, smooth and homogenous, lump-
less and liquid, pausing to recall her notes on the iniquity of
the English dairy system. She looked up: what demon possessed him, her youngest, playing on the lawn, demons and
angels? Why should it change, why could they not stay as they
were, never ageing? (She poured the mixture over the cherries in the dish.) The dome was now become a circle, the
cherries surrounded by the yeasty mixture that would cradle
and cushion them, the yeasty mixture that surrounded them all,
the house, the lawn, the asphodels, that devil Nicholas running
past the window, and she put it in a hot oven. In thirty minutes
it would be ready.

Fenkata

à la Homer

1 rabbit
2 onions
3 cloves of garlic
Extra virgin olive oil
10 fresh plum tomatoes, peeled
1 tablespoon tomato puree
Rabbit herbs (2 sprigs each of thyme and rosemary, and a
*   handful of flat-leaf parsley, all roughly chopped)*
75ml red wine
2 medium potatoes, peeled and chopped into small pieces
2 carrots, peeled and chopped
A handful of peas, preferably petit pois
2 bay leaves
Seasoning

Sing now, goddess, of the hunger of Peleus' son, Achilles. Tell me now, you Muses of Olympia, daughters of Zeus, of the empty-bellied Achaians, whose supplies were grown old and stagnant while they stormed the great walls of Ilion for ten long years. You who know all things, while we have heard only the rumour of it and know nothing, tell me now of the cunning of resourceful Odysseus who, when he saw the hunger that spread through the strong-greaved Achaians, as obliterating fire lights up a vast forest along the crest of a mountain, was not dismayed, but stood forward to take up his bow and his cauldron of bronze.

Now, when rosy-fingered dawn showed, Odysseus stirred from where he was sleeping and slung his bow over his shoulder. He bound the fair sandals beneath his shining feet and went on his way into the sand dunes. Soon he came upon a swift-footed coney grazing in the dunes, and now Odysseus the godlike, holding his bow and his quiver full of arrows, bent the bow before him and let the arrow fly. Nor was his aim untrue, but Apollo, who strikes from afar, was still angry with the strong-greaved Achaians and sent the arrow astray so that it fell harmlessly in the sand. Now the startled rabbit began to run to take cover, swiftly as a mountain stream, which gains speed before disappearing beneath the glistening rock, only to appear later in some unexpected place. But Athene appeared to Odysseus and told him to shoot a second arrow, though it seemed hopeless; and this time he did not waste his strength; the bronze-weighted arrow found its mark and passed through the liver and came out the other side and undid the strength of the rabbit's legs, and its black blood drenched the sand and its eyes were shrouded in darkness.

Odysseus bound the mighty creature's feet and slung him over his shoulder to carry back to the Achaians' camp on the beach of the grey sea, beneath the bows of the wooden ships.

Then swift-footed brilliant Achilles gave up his weeping and came out from his tent. He girt about his chest and loins a leather apron and skinned the rabbit and cut it expertly into equal parts. Then he took the pieces and fried them in olive oil until they were brown and the smoke rose up to high Olympus, where sit the gods who rule over men. Seeing Achilles the god-like no longer brooding in his tent, Menelaos took courage and came with herbs and seasoning, which he added to the caul-dron. Then resourceful Odysseus mixed the sweet wine in the bowl and poured it over the meat and removed the cauldron from the fire, to allow it to marinate for thirty minutes.

Atreus' son, wide-ruling Agamemnon the powerful, chopped the onions and shed tears, as a stream dark, running down the face of a cliff impassable, sheds its dim water; but raging that it was not king-like, he would chop no more. Now Achilles chopped the garlic and, in a separate cauldron given by Agamemnon, fried the onions and garlic, nor did he stop frying until the onions began to brown. Then he added the tomatoes, the puree, the vegetables and the bay leaves to heat and simmer for fifteen minutes. Now Nestor the wise, with the guidance of Athene, persuaded them to combine the contents of the two cauldrons into one. This they left to simmer over a cool part of the fire for one hour, so that the rabbit was soft and tender. Then Achilles offered up a prayer to mighty Zeus of the wide brows, and he poured the wine into the mixing bowl and looked up into the sky. "High Zeus in far Olympus, hear me as you have heard me before and did me honour and brought to pass the wish that I prayed for. For see how I myself have worked hard with my hands and cooked the rabbit and made offerings of the vitals. Grant that the food is good and that my work is appreciated by the Achaians, and not only when my hands rage invincible against the Trojans, and that the meal will be eaten in good spirit without dispute among the lords of the glancing-eyed Achaians." So he spoke in prayer, and Zeus of the wise counsel heard the son of Peleus and granted him one prayer but not the other. That the food should be good he allowed, but refused to let the meal pass in harmony.

But resourceful Odysseus was mindful of the appetites of the Achaians, and when the dish was ready he took the sauce to serve on platters over linguini as a starter. Now Agamemnon stood forward and claimed the biggest portion, "Since I am king and greater than all here so that no man may contend with me." He spoke thus and then sat down, and the anger came on war-like Achilles, so that his heart was divided two ways, whether to take up his sword and kill Agamemnon or whether to put aside his anger and serve him the worst portion. Then in answer spoke Achilles unto Agamemnon, lord of men. "You wine sack with a dog's appetite, my portion you threaten to reduce for which I laboured much. When the Achaians cook, do I have a share that is equal to yours? Though always the greater part of the cooking is the work of my hands, when the time comes to dispense the rations, yours is the far greater reward."

Now Nestor the horseman stood forth among them and spoke to them saying, "Proud Achilles, beyond others you are strong in battle, not one of all the Achaians will belittle your words nor speak against them, yet you have not completed your arguments. But let me speak, since I am older, and go through the whole matter, since there is none who can dishonour the thing I say. I will speak in the way it seems best to my mind, and no one shall have in his mind any thought that is better than this one that I have in my mind, either now or long before now. Let lots be shaken for all of you to see who wins which portion." So he spoke and each of them marked one lot as his own. They threw them in the helmet of Atreus' son Agamemnon. And Achilles set before each of them a portion, according to their lot. Nor was any man's hunger denied, and they put their hands forward to the good things that lay before them and ate until they had put away the desire for eating and drinking.

Vietnamese Chicken

à la Graham Greene

½ teaspoon grated lemon zest
3 cloves garlic
2 tablespoons fish sauce
1 tablespoon soy sauce
1 teaspoon finely ground black pepper
⅛ teaspoon cayenne
2 boneless chicken breasts
2 tablespoons dry sherry
2 tablespoons lemon juice
2 tablespoons peanut oil
1 teaspoon molasses

A recipe has no beginning or end: arbitrarily one chooses at what point the cooking instructions become necessary, after the butcher has done his work and before care of the dish passes to the seasoning whims of the guests. I choose the moment when, looking into the refrigerator, I noticed the naked white flesh of the chicken. As I stared at the breasts I felt a pain across my head. The sound of church bells announced even-song from across the darkening Common, and I sipped at a gin and tonic. The tonic was old and had lost its sparkle, leaving a bitter taste, but it was now too late to get anything fresher. The rain drove against the window, and water was collecting on the sill where it refused to close.

The smell of chopped garlic clung to my hands as I mixed it together with the lemon zest, fish and soy sauces, and the peppers, black and cayenne. The chicken breasts rested on the counter and my hand moved towards them as though guided by an unseen force. It was too late to go back; she would be here soon.

Ritually I sliced the breasts into thin strips. The white flesh lay on the plate like a shredded contract and I hurriedly threw it into the marinade. The soy and fish sauce splashed across the meat, like ink smudged in the wet. I covered the mixture and returned it to the refrigerator. Two more hours would be ideal, but if the chicken soaked for half an hour it would be all right. I thought that in future I must do better.

While the flesh marinated in the cold darkness I mixed together the sherry, molasses and lemon juice. I poured another gin, without tonic this time, and turned on the wireless. The choral music was interrupted by a reading, Psalm 51. I turned off the set, but I knew the reading and it continued silently in my head as I heated the oil in the wok until it was smoking.

I took the marinated breasts from the refrigerator and tipped them into the burning oil, turning them with a fork. When the chicken was almost ready I added the sherry sauce; the rich liquid thickening made a sharp contrast to the whiteness of the steamed rice I would serve with it. I had failed to wear an apron, and as I stirred more rapidly, the rich concoction splashed onto my white shirt. I wiped at it with a cloth but the stain grew worse. In my frustration I called out "Damned …", but before I could finish I was interrupted by a knock at the door.

Sole à la Dieppoise

à la Jorge Luis Borges

2 fillets of sole
½ litre mussels
100g button mushrooms
50g butter
125ml white wine
Half a lemon
1 tablespoon plain flour
Salt and pepper

The story that I shall tell concerns an incident that took place in London early in 1944. Its protagonist was proclaimed a hero by both sides of the conflict, yet its consequences favoured only one, and led to the downfall of a seemingly invincible tyrant with an insatiable appetite.

Early in the Second World War, fearing invasion, the British removed all signposts from their highways. The intention was that spies and invaders would find themselves lost in the endless labyrinth of Celtic curves that make up much of the British road network. The task of overseeing the project fell to Sir Henry Smith. Inspired by the British initiative, a Parisian restaurateur, Amadée Antonin, removed the place names from all dishes on the menu of his small hostelry. For a short while, German officers dining in Antonin's restaurant found themselves lost in a recondite menu without signposts. The entries for such dishes as Crayfish à la Bordelaise and Lobster à la Parisienne offered the diner no guidance as to the possible fates of the unfortunate decapods, and Paris Brest could only be ordered by those who had known the menu since childhood.

It was in the old Confitería Águila that I first came across Sir Henry Smith's story. A small item in the Buenos Aires journal *Carne y Producción* noted the anniversary of his death and gave brief details of his career. Later, during a lecture tour of Germany, I stumbled upon another report of Sir Henry Smith or of a second Sir Henry Smith. Here the story grew deeper and more complicated. The article concerned papers from the wartime government, only recently released, in which reference was made to Sir Henry as 'The Spying Knight of the Reich', German intelligence's highest-placed agent during the Second World War.

My lecture tour moved on to England and there I spent much of my free time researching the strange history of Sir Henry. From privileged access to the journal of his last days, written in the cuneiform he had learnt as Woolley's amanuensis at Sumerian Ur, I have tried to create a full picture of his final hours, faithful to the facts where they were available. As may be expected I will alter one or two details. Here is his story.

It was on 2 March 1944, at 1 p.m. precisely, that Sir Henry Smith turned into Great College Street and, before the chime of Big Ben had faded on the air, remembered the note that he had been handed as he left the House of Commons. Sir Henry read the single line that occupied the page. Fearing that he might faint, he steadied himself against a wall and refused an offer of help from a passer-by. The note was from his contact, Agent 42, who had recently been directing Sir Henry to pay particular attention to information that might indicate the location of a probable Allied invasion of France.

The imminent capture of Agent 42 inferred Sir Henry's own arrest and execution. In the few minutes required to walk home, and from the infinite choices that lay before him, Sir Henry decided upon his plan of action. From the small bookshelf in the kitchen he took down a little-thumbed volume and his glacial eyes began to scan the index: Cod à l'Anglaise, Cod Provençal, Crayfish à la Bordelaise, Fish Soup à la Nimoise, Sole à la Dieppoise. Satisfied, Sir Henry scribbled a note that he passed to the concierge with a large tip and instructions that the fish was not to be filleted.

Sir Henry, feeling the relief of a murderer who finds himself under arrest, sat on the sofa by the bookcase. He opened a volume at random and began to read. The pages told the story of Astyages, whose merciless numina had brought to him the rule of Persia, and who defined his invincible purpose through the dream interpretations of the Magi. On their advice Astyages ordered the death of his own grandchild. When his orders were frustrated by the disobedience of his general, Harpagus, Astyages butchered the latter's son and served him cooked to the nescient father. At the end of the meal the boy's head and hands were brought to the table. Harpagus made no show of revolt, but in secret sent a message, hidden in the stomach of a cooked hare, to Astyages' (now fully grown) grandson, Cyrus, promising the general's collusion in any attempt to overthrow the tyrant. Fearing discovery, Harpagus sent a second message, concealed in the boiled carcass of a turtle, urging all speed, which arrived before the first and gave rise to the apocryphal tale of the Greek fabulist.

The book grew heavy and Sir Henry fell into a sleep. He was visited by the same dream that had recurred at intervals over the preceding months. He found himself in a vast maze, whose creator was observing from a tower as the dreamer ran through the green corridors of the rain-drenched labyrinth, trying, unsuccessfully, to take an unseen direction or to make an unpredicted move. Sir Henry was awoken by the return of the concierge, whose trip had been a success. He left the minister with a pint of mussels and a single sole, with the spine still attached.

Sir Henry was neither an accomplished cook nor a habitual piscivore, but he prided himself that, as a loyal servant, he knew how to follow instructions. Opening the recipe book, he cleaned the mussels and left them to stand in a bowl of fresh water while he made a telephone call to a journalist on *The Times*. Reports tell us that the journalist agreed to come to Sir Henry's apartment at 8 o'clock that evening, on the understanding that the minister had a story for him. Sir Henry then seasoned the sole with salt and pepper and placed the pieces in a flameproof pan. The sun had by now descended below the rooftops and through the window he perceived the tower of

Westminster Abbey. The light of the gas flame took over from the extravagant sunset and illuminated Sir Henry's irremeable countenance. He drained the mussels and re-covered them with the fresh water so alien to their nature, discarding as irretrievable any that did not close when tapped. He fried the mushrooms in a little butter and squeezed some lemon juice over them, covering the pan to preserve the juices. Meanwhile, he re-drained the shellfish and placed the covered pan over a gentle heat, shaking it gently until all the bivalves were open, again removing any that did not conform with the majority. Sir Henry drained the liquid into a bowl and removed the mussels from their shells. The mushrooms were now ready and he poured the liquid from their pan over the sole, then added a glass of white wine and the juice from the mussels, so that there was just enough liquid to cover the fish.

Among the unread books in Sir Henry's library sat Augustine of Trieste's treatise on asceticism. Confronted with a meal of fish, Augustine postulates the argument against carnivorism. Once eaten, the fish would transubstantiate into the flesh of the anathematised eater, and, for Augustine, to whom this fish was Sir Henry's own ancestor, its consumption was no less than cannibalism. He brought the liquid to simmering point and poached the sole with measured chronometry. On the stroke of the eighth minute Sir Henry lifted the sole from the liquid and placed it onto a warmed serving dish. He surrounded the fish with the mussels and fried mushrooms and kept it warm while he reduced the poaching liquid by allowing it to boil for three minutes and 30 seconds. Meanwhile, Sir Henry facilitated the collaboration of the remaining butter and flour, which he interpolated gradually into the liquid, stirring continually until the sauce thickened. He thought of the infinite possibilities of these few ingredients and of the practicability of cookery being classified as a branch of mathematics, rejecting this hypothesis in favour of gastronomy as language. He poured the sauce over the fish and placed the dish under a hot grill for a few moments to brown, before serving it with mashed potato.

Debate concerning the actual ingredients employed is of a dialectical nature. The recipe book used by Sir Henry disappeared following the inquest but is likely to have been the spuriously modernised 1921 edition of *Baron Brisse's 366 Menus*. From the depositions of the concierge and of the journalist, I can hope to have reconstructed the recipe with a fair degree of accuracy.

Sir Henry poured a glass of white wine to accompany his meal, took the front door off the latch and sat down at the table. As the firmament grew dark and the Abbey disintegrated into the gloom, he conjectured that he would not have the honour of facing the opprobrium of his countrymen. The chimes of Big Ben could be heard as the clock struck the hour, and recalling other ancient evenings, Sir Henry offered up a short prayer before beginning his lustral supper.

He was found later that evening by the visiting journalist, his lean, athletic figure sprawled across the carpet, arms outstretched. On the table were the remains of a meal half-eaten and an open recipe book. The following day the late edition of *The Times* ran the headline MINISTER FOUND DEAD. Along with the title of the dish that he had been eating, the journalist had interpolated the detail that Sir Henry's throat had been lacerated by fish bones as he choked to death. Five days later a German infantry regiment was moved from the Normandy coast to a defensive position in the environs of Dieppe, and the first glowing obituaries had already appeared in honour of Sir Henry Smith.

Cheese on Toast

à la Harold Pinter

1 loaf of ciabatta
1 aubergine
Extra virgin olive oil
Pesto
200g mozzarella
2 teaspoons fresh oregano, chopped

ACT I

A kitchen, cluttered. A fluorescent tube is flickering. Beneath a window is a sink, piled with dirty dishes. The bin is overflowing with rubbish; nearby, empty bottles are standing. There is a small kitchen table; newspapers and unopened letters obscure the surface. At the table are two chairs. There is the sound of a key in a door, muffled voices. The door bangs shut; instantly HURLEY, a young man dressed in a leather jacket, and CLACK, an older man, tramp-like in appearance, enter stage left.

HURLEY. Come in, make yourself at home.
   (CLACK *enters and looks around.*)

Bloody light. I've been meaning to get a new tube.

(HURLEY *reaches up and taps the light with his finger until it stops flickering*.) I'll make you something to eat.

CLACK. I haven't eaten all day. I can't remember the last time I had a proper meal. I mean a proper sit-down meal, something hot.

HURLEY. (*Looking in the fridge*) Do you want to use the phone? Call your daughter?

CLACK. What, at this time? I'll call her tomorrow. She won't want to come up here tonight, she starts early in the morning.

HURLEY. I can't offer you much. I haven't done a proper shop for ages. How about cheese on toast?

CLACK. What sort of cheese?

HURLEY. Mozzarella.

CLACK. Mozza what?

HURLEY. Mozzarella. It's Italian.

CLACK. Not for me. I'll have a slice of toast though.

Pause

HURLEY. I must wash this grill sometime. (*He is holding a grill pan covered with dried cooked cheese. He cuts a ciabatta in half, lengthways. Similarly, he finely slices an aubergine and puts the pieces into a frying pan where some oil is heating*.)

CLACK. Not a bad little place you got here. All yours is it?

Pause

This must be worth a few bob. How long you been here?

HURLEY. I don't know ... about three years.

CLACK. Made a few bob on it, have you?

(HURLEY *puts the ciabatta under the grill to warm*.)

That's a big slice of toast.

HURLEY. It's ciabatta.

CLACK. Cia what?

HURLEY. Ciabatta. It's Italian bread.

CLACK. You Italian are you?

HURLEY. Everybody eats it these days: ciabatta, focaccia, schiacciata, panini.

CLACK. Can't you just put me a couple of slices in the toaster?

HURLEY. Toaster's broken.

Pause

I'd like to have a little Italian eatery one day. Nothing fancy, mind. Simple snacks: panini of ciabatta, focaccia, bruschetta; pasta lunches, spaghetti, penne, rigatoni; the basic sauces, pesto, Bolognese, arrabiata. Classic mains: carpaccio of tuna drizzled with truffle oil, pan-fried fillet of beef on a bed of wilted spinach in its own jus. You want a cup of tea with it?

CLACK. Now you're talking. A nice cup of tea.

HURLEY. You ever been to Italy? I knew a bloke there once, bit like you. That was years ago. He's probably dead by now. (*He removes the aubergine from the pan, the flesh has soaked up the oil and is a golden colour with dark stripes left by the ridges of the frying pan. The ciabatta has now warmed and he spreads a thin layer of pesto onto the cut side*). Where's your daughter live then?

CLACK. My what?

HURLEY. Your daughter. The one who was meant to pick you up at the station.

CLACK. Oh, her.

Pause

She lives in Catford.

HURLEY. Catford? I used to go to the dogs there. I remember one night I was doing well, nearly all winners I'd picked, till I put the lot on the last race. I did a forecast, two and four. I don't know why, I nearly always did two and four about. But that night I didn't. Only came in four and two. I lost the lot. You a gambler?

CLACK. What, and throw my money away like that? Not me.
(*Pause as he looks down at his lap.*)
You haven't got a safety pin have you?
(HURLEY *lays the slices of aubergine on top of the ciabatta and pesto and begins to slice the mozzarella.*)

HURLEY. You can give her a call in the morning. I'll make you a bed up.

CLACK. She works in the morning. I told you.

HURLEY. You like olive oil?
(*He lays the mozzarella over the aubergine, drizzles olive oil on top, and finally adds a sprinkle of chopped oregano, before placing the ciabatta under a hot grill.*)

CLACK. I don't want none of that foreign muck.

HURLEY. Olive oil? It's good for you.

CLACK. It's for cleaning your ears out, ain't it?

HURLEY. (*Drops a tea bag into the overflowing bin.*) Here you are, a cup of tea for you.

CLACK. (*Gives a sigh of contentment.*) You can't beat a nice cup of tea.
(*He sips at the tea and pulls a face.*)
You got any sugar?

HURLEY. Over there, on the table. I don't use it much.
(*The sugar has hardened. CLACK chips at it with a teaspoon until he has sweetened his tea enough. He checks it occasionally*

throughout the process. The sound of sizzling comes from the grill. HURLEY waits until the mozzarella has turned brown and golden in places.)

HURLEY. Here you are. It's ready.

(HURLEY *cuts the two lengths of ciabatta into pieces.*)

You'll try some, won't you?

CLACK. Not for me. That's no good to a man like me.

(HURLEY *puts the plate of ciabatta onto the table.*)

Don't look bad though, I'll give that to you. It's . . .

Pause

Well presented. That's what it is, well presented.

HURLEY. I would have done a salad garnish, or a few fresh basil leaves if I'd had them.

CLACK. Don't look bad at all.

Pause

I'll just have a taste.

(*He takes a piece and bites into it. The mozzarella sticks to his beard in long threads. His face brightens in surprise.*)

CLACK. That ain't bad, that ain't. I reckon you might make a go of that caff yet.

He reaches for a second piece. HURLEY is already eating. The two men sit in silence, occasionally sipping at their tea. The fluorescent tube begins to flicker again, but this time HURLEY ignores it. Lights slowly fade.

Curtain

Onion Tart

à la Geoffrey Chaucer

225g plain shortcrust pastry
1 tablespoon fresh thyme, chopped
25g butter
2 tablespoons olive oil
8 onions, finely sliced
Salt and black pepper
2 teaspoons caster sugar
¼ teaspoon each of grated nutmeg and ground ginger
2 eggs, plus 2 egg yolks
425ml double cream
Large pinch of saffron strands

Then spake oure Host.
"Now have we heard from every which one
Of our fellowship with receipts to tell, but one.
Maister Graham, as knoweth many a man,
Loves best tales of cuckoldry as he kan.
And thou, wyfe of Bloomesbury, long of face,
Right boldly hast thou taken thy place.

God knowes well thy stream of consciousnesse,
For your clafoutis may God you blesse.
And thou, clerke of Prague, put away thy bookes,
Tis no time for Ovid, our tales are for cookes.
Culinary are our metamorphoses,
From ingredients chaos, creators we.
And when such tellers as these turn their voices cleere,
To Ars Culinaria, as they have here,
Nourished are our Christian men's soules,
But no less our bellies, our board and bowls.
And thou, sire at excise, who hath herkened these tales,
All the while taking note and drinking ale,
Telle us some merry dish, by your fay,
For 'tis high time thou entreth in the play."
"Gladly", quod he,
"Certe I can roaste and seethe and broille and frye,
But, as it thinketh me, nought can best a pie.
Therefore I will go tell, as well as ever I kan,
A receipt that will nourishe us, every man.
Now herkneth what I saye.

Here beginneth the Man at Excise's receipt:
On a floured board roll pastry that it be thinne,
Caste thereto with thyme and line a deep tinne.
Trimme the edges neat with a cooke's knyfe,
Then bake it blinde at gasse mark fyve.
Melt the butter and oyle in an heavie panne,
Covered wiv a lidde, as knoweth every man.
Then adde onyons in slices fine ywrought,
And caste thereto sugar and salte.

Onion Tart

Cover the panne and turn the heat down low,
Stirre every while, else the onyons stick to.
Remove the lidde and seethe for ten minutes mo,
That the sauce reducteth and darke growe.
Strewe thereto nutmeg grated, tho keep some by,
And grounde gyngere, and return to the fyre.
Lightly beat the eggs and zolkes together,
And season wiv both salt and black pepper.
Heat the crème till just warme with saffron rich,
Then adde the beaten eggs for to mix.
Spoon the onyon sauce into the pastry case,
Then pour egg and crème custard into the base.
Bake in the oven for minutes xxv,
Til golden brown our tarte be."
"Now," quod our Host, "so God you blesse,
Ye have set an ensample for the rest,
Since ye so much knowen of that art,
And right well have you told us part.
Though in kitchen's cunning there's nought, dear brother,
That in olde tyme was not said by another,
In the way of telling your creation's made,
For none shall remember you by your trade.
Thy customhouse stores much of strange beauty,
And in future with tales will pilgrims pay duty."

Here endeth the receipt of the Exciseman of London.

Rösti

à la Thomas Mann

3 large grated potatoes, parboiled or if large floury sort,
  grated raw
1 onion, finely chopped
Cheese, Gruyère or Emmental
Salt and pepper to taste
Butter

Von Rohrbach felt himself in a state of strangely reduced vitality and was relieved to be at last gathering his strength in the air-conditioned interior. The morning walk had been overly ambitious and only now that he was at rest was he aware of the blood pounding in his temples and of his shortness of breath. His chest was heavy as he recalled the evil exhalations of the lunchtime traffic and resolved to avoid going abroad at such times as might prove inimical to his health.

The restaurant was well lit, elegant and comfortable. Feeling his fluttering pulse recover, Von Rohrbach ordered a glass of Gruaud Larose and sat back in the comfortable, high-backed chair to look about him. Luncheon was already under way and a queue was now forming at the entrance. Von Rohrbach glanced at the cringing waiter as he placed the glass before him. The waiter was a man of slight build, hardly of the Alsatian type, but tall and bony; the white linen tunic, unbuttoned at the neck, revealed the man's strikingly large Adam's apple and his servile manner made an unpleasant impression on the diner who was presented with a bound volume. A menu it apparently was, but a menu unlike any that Von Rohrbach had ever seen, indeed, compared to it, all other menus with which he was familiar seemed the briefest of notes, the vaguest of sketches; this was a menu devoid of any understanding for the hard-pressed diner, the adventurer wishing to be surprised, this was a menu that resembled the Treaty of Versailles in its scope and in its attempt to exclude all possibility of misunderstanding.

All his life Von Rohrbach had suffered from a sympathetic nerve in his solar plexus. It had afflicted his childhood and now caused him to skim over the pages of beef, pork and game – meats that might heighten his emotional energies or draw blood from the lungs to the heart. The ivory white of the paper calmed him, the rustle of the pages recalled his long hours in the studio. Lingering over the list of exotic dishes – he saw there a trout prepared after the manner of Pondicherry. He had never been to India, the travels of his youth had long since given way to the industry of his later years, the stern service that had brought its share of honours. It was he who had returned painting to its place of pre-eminence among the visual arts, who had renounced modernism and re-ignited the flame of German art. The menu's description wove in his mind a spell and summoned a picture. He saw, he beheld, a canvas; a group of fishermen returning from the river, around them the forest, thick with mangroves, their exposed roots reaching into the tidal stream, their nets full with an exotic catch, bug-eyed tiger prawns, flying fish brought to earth, spider crabs in their prehistoric armour; the fishermen triumphant, unaware of eyes that watch from the bamboo thicket where the tiger crouches. His brain reeled, his body still wet with sweat, Von Rohrbach sensed the danger, and closed the menu.

The tasteful interior began to fill with guests and the solitary diner released from his exotic study began to enjoy the scene before his eyes. That uniform of civilisation, the business suit, gave outward conformity to the varied types, but most of the principal European tongues could be heard within the confines of the restaurant. A Polish lady and her children were being served at the neighbouring table. They were about to eat when Von Rohrbach noticed with astonishment the perfect beauty of the vegetable accompaniment; that dish most popular in Switzerland but which finds itself reproduced in varying forms elsewhere in Europe: rösti. The rösti, its shape recalling the noblest moment of creation, the grated potato fried to form a cluster of honey-coloured ringlets, the centre thick and proud, golden, its edges burnt darker and tattered like the circumference of the sun, of a chaste perfection of form such that our diner felt his very entrails bewitched. The handsome young boy raised his knife and fork and, as he did so, first noticed the attentions of the older diner. The young lad's strange twilit grey eyes met those of the artist and Von Rohrbach saw, not without excitement, that his attentions were welcomed. As the boy's knife cut into the sweetly yielding centre of the golden disk the artist was utterly enraptured. Shamelessly he followed each mouthful and Von Rohrbach remarked exquisitely that the young lad did not betray him.

The rösti recalled a form and colour from his childhood that he could not place: the golden cluster, exquisitely framed by the viridian Dresden chinaware, the highly polished cutlery, like Narcissus' pool, reflecting the beauty of the dish. Time, which before had crept at a pace barely noticeable, now accelerated and with a stirring of regret Von Rohrbach saw that the beautiful young diner had reached the last few mouthfuls. A feeling of delicacy forced the painter to turn away, unwilling to witness the oily residue that would leave its stain on the surface of the plate.

The master sought the eye of the waiter. Once more time slowed and Von Rohrbach feared lest the kitchen be exhausted of its supply of the tuberous temptation. He sipped of his Gruaud Larose and eventually received the attentions that were his due, from a brutish-looking fellow whose lips curled back into a smile.

"I will have the rösti."

"Of course, sir, a speciality of the house; may I also recommend the blanquette de veau?"

Suspecting the waiter of trying to increase his tip Von Rohrbach refused, "Just the rösti ... and another glass of the Gruaud Larose."

He looked once more towards the youth to see if he had noticed the connection that was firmly established between them, but the lad was now in conversation with his sister. Time dragged for the artist, leader of the Romantic Expressionist movement, creator of the heralded work *Victor and Vanquished*, whose every painting was sold before the canvas had dried. There he sat. His eyes, now half-closed, signalling the vanity of the observer who refused to wear spectacles as he watched the doors of the kitchen. Waiters carrying empty dishes disappeared only to reappear, their arms charged anew with offerings from the sanctum, lesser priests who brought news from an unseen oracle to the faithful of the temple, devotees who had been to the very edge of the furnaces from which the sacrificed sent their smoky signals to the gods. A waiter emerged into the light pushing a heated trolley; to Von Rohrbach he appeared no less than Helios the sun god driving his chariot. The restaurant became the firmament and its crossing seemed to last an entire day. The flaming cargo fuelled the fires of the artist's appetite such that all appeared to hinder the passage of the celestial body until it found its resting place in front of the new acolyte, eagerly awaiting his initiation. There before him was laid the Gordian knot, whose solution lay, not in logic, but in the sword and the courage to sweep aside empires. Therein he saw the stellar and the terrestrial, how bewilderingly they mimic each other. The golden buckler lay on the smooth faience, its gilded coils glistening, recalling the reflection on the shield of Perseus.

Dazzled and beguiled, he took his blade and split the disk asunder. At the first mouthful his gaze found the strange twilit eyes of the youth and he was astonished anew – something between a pact and a promise had been established with the young pilgrim who had led him from darkness into light. The sensation was unmistakeable: there was cheese in the galette, surely no product of the valley floor but of higher ground, lofty eyries where hunts the eagle, a Gruyère perhaps or an Emmental. But there came further flavours; the sacred mingled with the profane, a taste from lower ground of onion mixed with the fruit of the new world. As a master mixes his oils in the studio, adding a little more ochre, a touch more vermilion until the balance is right, so Von Rohrbach now sought to penetrate the mysteries that found expression on his other palette. These potato shavings, natural yet incredible and uncanny, had been grated raw and seasoned to taste. Now, inextricably bound with the shredded onion and cheese, they had made the ascension from the subterranean to the extraterrestrial. This holy trinity had faced the fires of the pan together, cooked on a low heat in butter in a lidded pan for fifteen minutes on each side.

Beguiled, Von Rohrbach was reaching the last few morsels; in the final precious moments his eyes rolled upwards moving from side to side as though seeking something that can only be tasted from within. The maître d' had noticed his strange behaviour and instructed a waiter to present the bill; guests had been taken to the sanatorium before but it was not good for the establishment's reputation. Two more members of staff hurried forward and each taking an arm helped the diner from his table. Von Rohrbach's mouth hung open, his lips moved and he rehearsed the possible variations of rosti: "Sauté the onions first, fry with small pieces of bacon, replace the Gruyère with Gorgonzola ..." Half-carried, half-stumbling, he was led past the table where sat the lovely youth, and his eyes sought again that look of exquisite complicity. But the boy, now laughing as he shared dessert with his sister and mother, was unaware of the painter's departure. As the two members of staff deposited the trembling artist onto the street, a third removed the smeared plate and half-empty glass. To the Polish family, seated nearby, the table re-laid presented once more that perfect square of white linen which bears no trace of the artist's presence.

Moules Marinière

à la Italo Calvino

Mussels, approx. 500g per person
50g butter
4 shallots, chopped
1 clove garlic
100ml white wine
A sprig of fresh thyme
25g fresh flat-leaf parsley
Pepper to taste
Cream (optional)
Bay leaf (optional)

I write this recipe without knowledge of when or where it will find an audience, but now, reader, you are here. What form this account takes I cannot say; perhaps you have found a manuscript in the attic of your new home and your curiosity has been aroused, or perhaps the recipe has found its way into print in a periodical or even in the hard shell and respectability of a book. You may already have searched the pages for an indication as to its author, who, perhaps, has already tasted the recipe for the last time, while you, reader, approach it for the first. Mercifully, recipes are not perishable in the same way as food or writers, although if Aristophanes wrote recipes, they have not kept as well as his plays.

It is quite likely that you are planning a meal, unless you are one of that small coterie that reads recipes in bed late at night. Readers of recipes are fickle and a reader such as you certainly has other books on cookery to hand. Without doubt you have already discarded a number of other recipes as unsuitable:

recipes for which you have not the right equipment; a fish kettle is expensive and difficult to store in your small kitchen;

recipes that are too laborious – the Athens of Aristophanes was run by slaves and the preparation of dormice is long;

recipes too critical in their timing;

recipes unacceptable on religious or moral grounds: pork, dolphin, dog;

recipes that have become redundant. Such is the ease of the ready-made, who now makes jam, bread, pastry (puff pastry least of all)?

But is this the recipe you are seeking? Without doubt you have read the title and are open, at least in principle, to the idea of moules marinière. You have cast an eye over the ingredients and it now seems that if you can find mussels, the preparation will present few difficulties, but your decision will be made at the last minute, according to market price and availability.

Moules Marinière

You have returned, then. The trip to the fishmonger was a success. At the last moment you were perhaps tempted by the bright eyes of a fish, but you remembered your fear of bones, small, white and sharp, perfectly disguised in the white flesh. *Mytilus edulis* conveniently wears his skeleton on the outside where we can see it. It comes off in two neat pieces, leaving the little jelly-like body defenceless. But for the moment the black molluscs lie on the draining board and, like armoured troops awaiting their orders, they must be made clean, and present-able. With a knife and under a cold running tap you remove any traces of weed, barnacle or other small crustacea that might be inhabiting the black skeletons of our bivalves.

So now the mussels are clean, each shell black and shining as a hearse. The mourners are crammed into a pan and covered with fresh water. Outside the sound of chopping alarms them – you have begun work on the shallots. Perhaps the guests are here already. Don't allow them to distract you; leave them to drink their aperitifs in another room, or better still ask a guest to chop the parsley while he drinks his glass of chilled Muscadet – that way you can concentrate on other details. What will you serve with the mussels? The oven is hot, but you don't want the guests to see the oven chips poured from the plastic bag; the magic might be broken. Send them away. You knew it was a mistake to let them into the kitchen; the oven is not even hot. If the dish is a starter send one of them to the bakery for a baguette or two.

In a large pan, one for which you have a lid, the chopped shallots are now sizzling in the melted butter with the thyme, perhaps even a bay leaf. You add the garlic, chopped finely. Now inspect the mussels. Reject any that remain open. Like books on a shelf they must all be closed. Like writers, they do not welcome visitors; a tap on the shell and it closes tighter than a priest's breviary. Now cast them into the pan and add the white wine. As the liquid falls onto the hot oil it makes a hissing sound and steam rises. The guests are impressed. You replace the lid and the noise dies down; in five minutes it will be ready. Are the bowls warm? Is the table prepared? Are there candles, wine, wine glasses? The stage must be set. Perhaps you are eating alone. Still there is no harm in making the table a pleasant place to sit. Reading a book is difficult when there are mussels to be eaten; instead you play some quiet music.

The lid of the pan is jumping: the meal is nearly ready, its author almost forgotten. Do you now add the fresh parsley? How much? How soon? You cannot recall and the guests are watching. Having memorised its contents you have hidden the incriminating recipe, and the guests suspect nothing. "A little dish of my own, handed to me by my grandmother … I improvised." The author is one of many ingredients that can be left out at the time of serving. Confess you have been unfaithful to my text, my own fault, "pepper to taste" showed the weakness which inspired the revolution. There are no shallots? Then onion will do. If we added cream it would be more of a treat, and let's not bother with the thyme. Does a writer of recipes not deserve the same respect as other authors? Do his writings not depend for their creativity on the most subtle of inventions, a well-placed grain of salt, delicate variations of flame and heat? You would not dream of treating writers of "literature" in such a way. *What*? Raskolnikov kills her with an axe? Too violent, a blunt instrument will do: let us say she is knocked unconscious with a rolling pin.

Moules Marinière

The guests are at the table, there is time to check the recipe once more. You take the book from the shelf one last time for reassurance, only this time the recipe calls for a bouquet garni … it should have gone into the pan with the onion and shallots. But wait, this is not the same book … you can hear the guests' voices in the next room, you take down another volume. Moules marinière: yes, there it is, but you now note that the final lines require you to "Add the cream". There was no mention of cream … you have no cream. Your guests call from the dining room – can they help? "Stay there," you cry. You do not want be seen reading from a book. "It's nearly ready. Choose some music." Where is the original recipe for moules marinière? What is this dish that you have made? What use is a recipe that keeps changing? But wait, this is not the right book. In fury you throw the volume into the empty sink. You would throw it into a pan of boiling water, letting it bubble until it is no more than a thin porridge; or better still you would like to grate it until a pile of shredded paper sits on the work surface. Some words might still be legible and you will settle for nothing less than complete annihilation. You pass them through the mincer, the blender, the liquidiser, so the book becomes so much confetti. You might grind them with pestle and mortar to produce a flour from which you will bake bread and feed it in morsels to migrating birds. Better yet, spread the tiny flakes of print on a pan and scorch them under a hot grill. You envisage the smoke as it begins to rise but the sinuous forms take on the appearance of letters, then words, an affront to your efforts. Let the extractor fan do its work and watch the smoke drawn up, expelled and dispersed into the atmosphere as the tiniest particles, rising beyond the city to be carried off on the four winds. You want to do this, but there is no time, the guests are hungry. Then on another shelf you notice the broken spine. In your haste you have placed the original recipe book not on the shelf reserved for cookery books, but on that allocated to literature. You take one last look, you have only to add the parsley, fresh, flat-leafed, roughly chopped. Cream is optional. You return the book to the same place on the shelf, next to the works of Italo Calvino, and serve.

Plum Pudding

à la Charles Dickens

4oz suet, finely chopped
4oz raisins
4oz currants
4oz plain flour
Pinch of salt
1 rounded teaspoon baking powder
4oz breadcrumbs
4oz moist sugar
¼ teaspoon ground mace
¼ teaspoon grated nutmeg
1 egg
1 gill milk (approx.)

The Judge's Chamber – A Christmas Tale

THE FIRST TRIAL

The Artful Dodger was dead, of that there could be no doubt. His brief light had shone brightly on Jacob's Island and in the unlit streets of Bermondsey and Rotherhithe, where many had made him their model. And oh, he had made them laugh when he stood in the dock, for Fagin had said he would never peach, not the Dodger, even if he were for the drop, and he never did. But Fagin was dead, stretched a week before, so it was the transports for the Dodger. His passage, HMS *Penitent* had gone down in rough seas. Captain and crew had abandoned ship, but the cargo had not been saved, and the cargo was prisoners, flesh and blood, men and boys, chained and shackled, and the great weight of iron had dragged them down and the Artful Dodger had sunk where there were no snuff boxes, nor candlesticks, nor silverware, nor bright kerchiefs, and the Dodger's nimble hands lay among the coral where denizens of other depths picked at him, until he had no more to give. The Artful Dodger was dead, and the newspaper, that Christmas Eve, was as good as a death certificate in the cosy chambers wherein his honour, Justice Hungby, warmed himself by the fire, with his coffee and his toasted muffin, in anticipation of the last case of that year 1842. One of that bad lot, a boy, was to stand that morning before the judge's bench, charged with the violent robbery of items necessary for the concoction of a plum pudding and without doubt, a worthy subject for transportation in the impartial eyes of Tobias Hungby.

"Dism, there seems abroad a morbid and sickly sentimentality about young criminals accompanied by a want of feeling towards the victims of their sins. I trust you do not share it?" The comment was addressed to his clerk, a pathetic fellow who was engaged in removing the carcass of a fly from the windowsill. The clerk, holding the fly by those appendages so essential to the transport from which it derives its name, shook his head while Judge Hungby took a bite of his muffin and a mouthful of coffee. He had booked a good many passages on the *Penitent* and shown as little interest in the welfare of those he sent on their way as he showed now that their voyage had come to its brutal end.

The judge was undistracted from his reading by the chimes of the clock, which was decorated in holly and ivy in token of the season, until, at the eighth bell, the sound turned wet and he saw a drip land with a small splash, and a large measure of impudence, on the green leather inlay of his desk-top. Looking up in the spirit of inquiry for which the legal profession is so well known, he saw that a stain had appeared on the ceiling, dark brown in colour and seeming to grow larger by the second. The clerk was summoned, blamed and sent to investigate. The judge read on, taking in several pages of the utmost depravity: an unidentified body washed up by the Thames at Wapping, escaped convicts prowling the Woolwich marshes, a prostitute bludgeoned to death in her lodgings. By way of variety the paper reported the story of a suicide who had drowned himself by tying a bucket to his head before diving into a canal, and it entered the judge's mind to consider what sentence he would have given the scoundrel had the attempt failed. Prison was so often a poor deterrent; it was well known that prisoners were better fed than the law-abiding poor. The judge took another bite from his muffin and pondered the solutions to the tide of crime that threatened to engulf the city – a course of meditation that on this occasion was brought to a halt when a drip struck him squarely on the forehead. With all the authority of his position he glowered at the leak and struggled to suppress a shiver as he now remarked a striking resemblance of the dark patches on the ceiling to the eyes and mouth of a skull. From the mouth the drips had become a steady stream whilst the drops from the eye sockets might have been mistaken for tears.

The water now began to rise and the judge, making to leave the room, found this to be an action more easily projected than done, for the door was now locked. With a growing sense of dread his fingers rattled the knob, his mouth began shouting for the clerk and his fists attacked the door with a savagery usually reserved for his judgments. The fire that had kept the judge's chambers so warm on this cold December day now hissed and spat, before succumbing to the icy flood. Trapped and with the water still rising Judge Hungby made for higher ground. His feet splashed through the dark water, as he stepped first onto his chair and thence onto the desk where he crouched hugging his knees and awaiting the return of the clerical dipterist. The waters gave no sign of abating and were now nearly at the height of the desktop, about which they seemed to be flowing in a circular motion as though the island sat at the centre of some nefarious whirlpool. Holding his hands over his face the judge called again for the clerk, but could not keep his eyes from the dark surface of the water, or his imagination from the flotsam that bumped about the wooden island. The island's inhabitant now grew silent, his eye drawn by anything that moved on the current, his ear by flotsam unseen in the gloom as it bumped against the furnishings and panelling of the chamber. With absorbed attention he now eyed some peculiar item of debris whose identity defied him. The realisation that it was a half-submerged clump of grey hair caused the blood to drain from the judge's face and, were he given to fancy, might have made his stomach to turn a somersault, but he was not. The superior power of his forensic mind prevailed and Hungby stretched out an arm to retrieve his old barrister's wig, but before he could touch the reverend horsehair his arm froze, his eyes widened, and the scant strands rose, as best they could, on his head.

There in the water floated a body, face down, its grey flesh and bloated proportions testifying that it had long been submerged.

In that agony of fear he could not take his eyes from the corpse, carried as it was on the dark flood. The sound of dripping echoed in that little chamber like the ticking of a clock and in the darkness the corpse seemed to glow like a bad oyster. Its black hair swayed like seaweed on the water's surface as the current brought the floating form closer to the desk where, to the judge's horror, its head came to rest with a heavy bump inches from the saucer-like eyes of our terrified castaway.

Like little bells the chains that hung from the ankles and wrists of the body tinkled in the water and revealed the status of the bearer. A large drip fell from the ceiling, and landed with a splash on the corpse's scalp. As though woken from its deathly slumber the corpse raised its watery countenance whence grey eyes met the judge's petrified gaze.

"My snuff's all wet, you wouldn't ave a pinch would yer?"

The judge's blood stood still and a trembling took hold of every limb as the spectre, for how could it be else, came to life.

"Don't you look at me like that, after all it was you what put me in this disgraceful sitivation. Don't I deserve to be lagged on land? Not left to drown in a stinking 'ulk."

The judge was now racked by the most awful chattering of his teeth and seemed to have lost all power of speech.

The phantom continued, "Speak up, man. Guilty or not guilty, 'ow do you plead?"

Seeing the judge's mouth open and close soundlessly the corpse smiled. "Enough of your games, you old scoundrel. Don't you know me?"

Despite its terrible aspect, there was something of the apparition's snub-nosed physiognomy that yet dwelt in the judge's recollection.

"The old Artful Dodger? I was to be the greatest of my time. Didn't the gaffer 'imself say so? Worth fifty times the tuppenny halfpenny snuff box what you lagged me for. Oh, but you could teach the gaffer a thing or two, I'll bet you made a bit of blunt a sending of boys on the transports."

By now the judge was whining and mumbling incoherently.

"Make a note, clerk, the prisoner refuses to reply."

The Dodger was enjoying his part. Now floating on his back he had taken up the judge's wig from the waters to place it dripping above his own flattened brow and taking hold of the lapels of his jacket he was now affecting the learned air of self-satisfaction so familiar in the courts.

"Oh, ladies and gentlemen, we 'ave before us a proper villain. A villain not on the outside, but the worst of all, a villain on the inside with an 'art as black as his gown."

The Dodger looked well pleased with his eloquence and

with a great rattling of chains set to swimming backstroke, the irons on his bowed legs chiming like the tolling of a ship's bell.

"Oh, your honour," said the counsel aspirating the h, "These irons is 'eavy. But they were 'eavier still when I was alive and suffering from the fever."

The prosecutor paused at this revelation to see what effect it wrought on the defendant, who had begun to sob out of pity for himself.

"Tears in the court? You won't fool me, you old cur. Call the first witness."

The Dodger's voice reverberated in the chamber as though it were some vast cavern. As the echo died the door of the judge's closet swung open causing a small wave on which the floating counsel bobbed contentedly. Outside snow was falling and a faint glimmer of light reflecting off the surface of the water revealed a man suspended by a noose from the back of the door. The floating prosecutor now addressed himself to the corpse, its mouth agape and its tongue protruding almost onto its chest. "Could my learned friend look around this 'ere room."

It was a habit of Judge Hungby's to find fault with the procedure of counsel and, notwithstanding the dread and trembling that currently occupied his mind and body, he did so now.

"You have not sworn the witness." There was a note of desperation in his usual measured tones.

"Swear 'im? The gaffer? A 'spectable old genleman of his reputation? 'E ain't any cause to lie. Any road I'll 'ave you for contempt."

The witness raised its face, terrible to behold, revealing the rope which cut deep into the throat and neck; its eyes bulged and a white foam lay upon its lips. It made a rattling sound as though clearing its throat and then spoke.

"Dodger, my dear, you will be the greatest lawyer of the age."

"Thank ee, Fagin. Can you tell the court, in your own words, *Mr* Fagin, the particklers of the crime."

"Yes, my dear, I was minding my own business, a planning of your release, when that villain put this rope about my neck and sent me for the drop. Oh, ladies and gentlemen of the court I did suffer in extremest." The hanged man then pulled a stream of colourful handkerchiefs from his pocket, all tied in a row, and held one end to his eye, whilst being sure to watch the effect they had on the court as he half-sobbed, half-choked

"Try to compose yourself, Mr Fagin, look around this 'ere room and tell the court if you can you see 'im what put that rope around your neck and stretched you so piteously?"

The terrible eyes of the hanged man made a great show of looking in all directions before alighting on the judge, at which the dread countenance broke into a decayed grin.

The phantom raised a bony hand, its fingers protruding from the fingerless glove of faded black and indicated the judge, now coiled so tightly in his robe that he resembled a large beetle with a human head.

"That's 'im," said the pendant witness, "a more blood-thirsty devil, or a tidier murderer I've never seen."

The judge renewed his sobbing, his face had taken on the unwholesome grey phosphorescence of the phantoms that now tormented him and there broke out upon his lips a curious grey foam, like day-old snow, as he whimpered in appeal, "But he deserved to die." Fagin opened his eyes and mouth wide at the Dodger as though his worst crime had been to borrow a cup of sugar and not to return it.

"The witness is not on trial," said the Dodger with a yawn, as if this old ruse were tried every day. "And don't address me, man, address the jury." He began to chuckle, still swimming playfully on his back. A smell of sulphur filled the chamber as the defendant looked around the room for evidence of the committee in question. He heard the voice of the prosecutor, "Gentleman of the jury, 'ave you reached your verdick?"

"Hold your noise." There came a deeper voice from within the chamber and from the shadows stood forth a huge man dressed in the coarse cloth of the prison, the arrows painted on his clothes pointing upwards as if to draw attention to his massive head, in which his one eye, half-closed, seemed to be winking. His nose was almost flat and its irregular contours suggested that it had been incompletely and unskilfully flattened with a blunt instrument, and the figure's horrific aspect was made the more disturbing by the presence on his head of a judge's forensic wig. The man, or spectre, or demon climbed up onto the desk and made the defendant stand. Anyone could see that Judge Hungby shook with fear as he leant on the spectre to support his trembling legs. A noose fell from the darkness above and hung before the judge's face. While the condemned man begged for clemency, and promised an end to transportation, the huge convict tied the judge's arms, fastened the noose about his neck and then stepped down into the water to join company with his fellow phantoms. As though through a picture frame the judge caught a last glimpse of the three officials of the court. Waist deep in water they looked back at him. The Artful Dodger and the Convict removed their wigs to bow, Fagin, meanwhile, with one hand held up the end of the instrument of his own demise and curtsied, in a movement seldom seen but graceful to behold. The three accomplices then placed their hands on the desk, braced their bodies, and, as the dodger called aloud "Heave!", the great mahogany desk began to move. Two more heaves and the judge teetered on its edge, unable to gain any purchase. He struggled for a few moments before his feet gave way and he dropped. The tightening noose cut short his scream and with a terrific convulsion of the limbs Tobias Hungby lost consciousness.

THE SECOND TRIAL

"Sir, the court is waiting." The clerk's hand on Judge Hungby's shoulder woke him, the morning newspaper lay on his lap, the heat of the fire burnt his cheek, the clock on the mantelpiece, dressed still with holly and ivy, chimed the o'clock as the judge put his hand to his throat.

"Dism," he addressed the clerk, "what day is it?"

"Why it's Christmas Eve, sir," the clerk addressed the judge.

"Then there has been no inundation of my chambers?"

"No, sir, the leak was occasioned by the clerks above, sir, upturning a jug of porter in premature high spirits of the season."

"Then I have not been on trial for my life. O glorious day, o wonderful clerk, Dism, o season of joy, quick, quick help me into my gown!" Judge Hungby examined his forensic wig, as though he now held it for the first time, before placing it over no great quantity of hair, and showing an expression of such contentment that I doubt has ever been seen beneath that token of authority in general and I am certain had never been seen beneath that token in particular, he addressed his clerk with, of all things, a smile. "The case, Dism, o wonderful boy, what is this morning's glorious business?"

"A series of robberies, your honour, with violence. A boy, stealing from a grocer's and fruiterers," the clerk replied.

"Poor boy." There was a smash as the clerk dropped the coffee cup that he was removing. "Hunger, Dism, is a terrible thing. Would that Famine might stand one day before me in the dock. Now is the season to chase him from the world." And with that he ran from the chamber, leaving the clerk gathering the pieces of broken crockery.

The courtroom could hardly have been more crowded had Famine indeed been on trial in Judge Hungby's court that Christmas Eve. Outside the sun struggled to make himself known from above the cloud that had settled over Holborn and the city, and could do little to raise the temperature on such a cold December morning. The clean white snow sat high up on the rooftops and dripped down into the dirty snow that lay in the streets and found itself churned and begrimed by the passing traffic. Shoppers performed like circus entertainers as they carried improbable numbers of parcels, and grocers and poulterers watched queues form as they struggled to cope with the demand at this time when all eat more heartily than on any other day of the year. Yet some still found leisure to fill the gallery for a chance to see the guilty pay for their crimes, or to warm their hands and feet before the spectacle of the law. A young boy of eight or nine years of age stood in the dock, his face so wan, so prematurely old, like so many of his kind. Only a wooden crate enabled the little creature to be seen behind the iron spikes that served to keep such ferocious creatures from the good men of the bench.

Mr Bisquiz appeared for the prosecution. He had a small mouth and eyes, and whiskers that struggled to grow in the hard ground of his countenance so that his face seemed decidedly underfurnished. His angular body was similarly sparse and appeared, with all of its sharp angles, to be ideally suited to the prising open of sealed containers. Bisquiz's techniques rarely failed in the court of Judge Hungby and he painted a dark picture of young Tom White, the prisoner. He might appear young in years, Bisquiz argued, but he was old in the crime of the streets, and that the crime for which he appeared in the dock today was unlikely to be his first offence and even less likely to be the most serious of offences that lay behind or before him.

The shopkeeper, Mr Tartberry, was called to the witness box. A well-fed gentleman with red hair, redder cheeks and a black eye took the stand. He was sworn and then stood twisting his hat as though wringing water from wet laundry, till finally overcome by the attention of the court, he stared down at his boots. On being pressed, Mr Tartberry described his long suffering at the hands of the accused and of his fellows, writhing and groaning with each grievance in such a way as gave the court to understand that his losses had been severe and might well have included the theft of some one or more of his vital organs.

"I was serving one of the ladies of the neighbourhood, Mrs Chickenstalker it were, with some of my finest Norfolk Biffins when I saw the boy place a handful of raisins in his one pocket and a handful of currants in the other."

"A great quantity of dried fruit would you say, Mr Tartberry?"

"I should say, about four ounces of each, sir."

"Did you then challenge the thief?"

"I did, sir, though I was struck dumb when I saw him place a quarter pound packet of flour into his trousers. I am not so young as I was, but I excused myself from Mrs Chickenstalker and wasted no time in chasing the prisoner. But boys can be awful quick, sir."

"Did he flee the premises?"

"He did, sir, he fled all around them premises, while I chased him and Mrs Chickenstalker attempted to lay her bag on him. She's a powerfully built woman, sir, and would have killed him outright for sure with one blow of her shopping bag, and spared us all a morning in court."

"No doubt the two of you proved sufficient to see off the juvenile?"

"No, sir, the little wretch was not leaving until he had all he wanted. He ran alright, not out, but round the shop, a holding onto his hat and looking about him until he snatched up a quarter pound of moist sugar from the counter."

"The scene must have been most distressing for you, Mr Tartberry?"

"I'll say, the boy would've murdered me with running

after 'im if Mrs Chickenstalker's shopping bag 'adn't laid me out like a like a blow from the blacksmith's 'ammer."

A policeman was then called to describe the circumstances of the arrest. Following Mr Tartberry's complaint and the theft of four ounces of suet and an egg from a nearby butcher's shop, the police had forced an entry into a building in Calthorp Street, whereupon a motley crew of men, women and boys had fled the building by window and rooftop, some few escaping over the wall that stood at the back of the residence. The house was deserted except for the prisoner who was found in the basement tending a pudding.

"And is it true, officer, that you did find the paper I have here in my hand constituting a confession and projecting a more serious attack on Mr Tartberry's premises?" Pressed to reply with a yes or a no the policeman had no alternative but to reply in the affirmative.

"I hold here in my hand a scrap of paper upon which has been written, 'Mace and Nutmeg'. I hesitate to encourage the ladies and gentleman of the court to imagine what violence our young plotter intended for Mr Tartberry and those who would stand in his way. Harmless he may look, but I never saw a juvenile more bound for the gallows. Who here would care to see the prisoner at liberty, armed with mace and ready to nutmeg us in our beds for a pound of raisins?"

The prisoner's large eyes peered over the side of the dock as he struggled to recognise himself in this portrait. He had suffered a good many beatings in his short time but never had he been able to give the same in return, not even with the aid of the aforementioned instruments.

*

Anticipating the judgment, more people had filled the gallery and newcomers feeling the warmth of the courtroom removed their snow-covered hats and comforters. Habits long held die hard and despite the charitable spirits with which he had opened proceedings, Judge Hungby was growing impatient. His court had seen men condemned to hard labour on less evidence than this. The prosecution's case was made and lunch was beckoning when, from a comforter which had been left to hang from the gallery, some melting snow fell onto the courtroom floor. The splash landed within earshot of the wigged authority and caused that instrument of justice no small consternation. At almost the same moment there came an almighty crash in which Judge Hungby imagined that he heard also the rattling of chains in the hold of a ship and the sound of the tide breaching a bulkhead. Fearing the worst the judge fell to his knees imploring the unseen force to spare him.

"Your honour, the boy seems to have fainted." It was the policeman who spoke to the now cowering judge.

"What?"

"The boy, sir, he's half-starved."

"The boy? Fainted? Wonderful news." An expression of relief suffused the judge's face, as he hurriedly prevailed the policeman to help him up from the floor. "Poor boy, I mean. Officer, take him through to my chamber."

The shopkeeper, blinking, stood now the sole object of the court's attention and tried to affect a relaxed expression.

"Mr Tartberry." The judge addressed the witness.

"Your honour?" The witness addressed the judge.

"You have had ample opportunity now to view the defendant, have you not?"

"Yes, I have, your honour."

"And on this occasion the defendant was stationary, was he not?"

"Begging your pardon, your grace."

"I mean, he did not run away."

"No, sir, not this time, 'e couldn't."

"More time to study him, would you say, than on the occasion of the theft from your premises."

"Oh yes, indeed, sir."

"So it would be fair to say that you now have a very good idea of the appearance of the boy in question."

"Oh yes, your worship, I'd know 'im anywhere."

"Excellent, excellent, Mr Tartberry. Would you then describe him to the court."

The grocer, surprised by the sudden turn of events, showed the expression of a man who has just realised that his purse is missing.

"I will not hurry you," said the judge, hurrying the witness.

"Well, 'e was small, small for his age I would say, with a cunning roguish look in 'is eye."

"I have a pretty large experience of boys and they're a bad set of fellows at that, but that they are small, with a roguish look, would appear to be an aspect common to all boys. Mr Tartberry, for the benefit of the court, could you describe this boy in *particular*."

"Quick 'ands 'e 'ad, and deep pockets and no respec' for 'is elders, like the rest of his gang."

"Thank you, Mr Tartberry, but in what respect did he differ from the rest of his kind?"

The grocer, who could have told a currant from a raisin, an orange pekoe from a ceylon, a wax candle from tallow, seemed unsure of how to tell one boy from another.

"Would you tell us what colour were his eyes, or the colour of his coat?"

Mr Tartberry hesitated.

"I have no wish to hurry you, but the range of colours is not great."

"They were blue, a cold blue." The witness bit down hard on the side of the knuckle of his index finger and thinking better of his words, "A green blue, with touches of hazel. And he wore a green coat."

Judge Hungby's face beamed, surprising all who were familiar with his manner and suggesting that the witness's precision had now secured a rapid conviction and an early lunch.

"Usher, would you bring the defendant back into the court."

There was a general gasp as the boy returned, his head bowed, his too long sleeves covering his hands; he stepped up onto the box to be seen by the court. His brown coat was faded and tattered unlike the rich brown of his eyes that gazed out fearfully on all the majesty of the law.

At this manifestation of the shopkeeper's error, a great roar rose up from the gallery and broke like a wave upon the court and over its foam and surf came the judgment of Hungby: "Case dismissed! Tartberry, bring the pudding."

THE THIRD TRIAL

So clerk and counsel, judge and gaoler, prisoner and police-man gathered in the judge's chamber. Tom took his place at the table where sat the pudding, and Mr Bisquiz inquiring as to its manufacture learned how Tom had sifted the flour, salt and baking powder and had mixed these with breadcrumbs, suet, dried fruit, sugar and spices.

"Does that not make for an awful dry mixture?" inquired the judge.

"No, sir, not once I added the egg and milk and mixed it well. Please, sir, then I turned it into a well-greased basin, which I covered and steamed for five hours."

And old Bisquiz, holding up his portion before the lamp to examine its colour, and poking and prodding its surface to test its texture, finally consented to place a morsel in his too hollow cheek where he could find no false note in the flavour of the pudding. And even Tartberry, who was in no small hurry to return to his busy shop, allowed that if they were his dried fruits then they were put to uncommon good use and that he might shift a good many of the puddings next season if Tom White had a mind to make them with good ingredi-ents, honestly come by. And all agreed that there had never been a better pudding nor a better Christmas Eve. And the ruddy, brown-faced, broad-girthed pudding sat and gleamed to hear itself talked of in such terms, shining in the fatness of its new steamed glory and urging and beseeching one and all to share in its eating. As for Judge Hungby, looking on as his companions laughed and feasted about the same desk upon which, only that morning, he had feared to breathe his last, he could find in his heart no word of criticism for the pudding, that he judged to be a good one. In such company even Dism caught a taste of optimism for the new year, and young Tom, who had never before sat among such genteel folk was so exceedingly grateful for his deliverance from the charges, for the warm fire at his back and for the laughter that shook the judge's desk, but most of all for the rich, sweet comforting taste of the plum pudding, one mouthful of which was as good a safeguard against hunger and low spirits as a man can hope for, that he cried aloud, "God bless us, every one."

Great Writer's DIY Tips

Hanging Wallpaper

with Ernest Hemingway

TOOLS:
Pasting brush
Wallpaper brush
Decorator's scissors
Pasting table
Plumb line

MATERIALS:
Wallpaper
Wallpaper paste

The old man had worked for two days and two nights to strip away the old wallpaper and now on the morning of the third day the time to hang the new paper had come and he was tired. His palms were blistered from long hours scraping away the old paper and the blisters had begun to weep. The old man felt the pain in his hands as he looked again at the bare walls of the room. "Room, thou art big. But I will finish this *trabajo* that I have begun," he said. "Or I will die trying."

The old man held the line delicately in his right hand. He threaded it through the eye on the lead weight, then he made fast the end of the line to hold the weight in place. The lead weight pulled firmly now and as he let the line run through his fingers he raised his arms so that the weight did not touch the ground, and the line remained taut and straight. Now he was ready. His right hand holding the line between thumb and forefinger, the left feeding the line, the old man raised his hands and climbed the first of the steps and offered the line to the wall where it swung like the pendulum of a clock. He could feel the tension on the line as it swung and he waited patiently. "It is losing momentum, soon it will circle and stop," he thought. Then he felt the weight go still and saw that the line hung straight between heaven and earth, and the old man took the pencil from behind his ear and drew a mark on the wall beside the plumb line.

The brown wall was patched with plaster and board, and the old man drew the line from ceiling to skirting board. As he drew, he descended the ladder, step by step, but always he held the line tight to the wall. Then the old man shouldered the first roll of wallpaper and carried it to the pasting table where he uncoiled the paper, pattern downwards, on to the wooden surface. As he unrolled the paper he bent low, his arms out straight, his palms turned up, until his face touched against the surface. Then he used two pieces of wood to stop the paper from rolling up on itself, one lengthways, one sideways.

He climbed the steps again and with the tape he measured the height of the wall from ceiling to skirting board. He wore rope-soled shoes, dark trousers and an old shirt. His shirt was patched and discoloured, and it resembled the wall. At the pasting table he loosened his sheath knife and cut the first drop three inches longer than the wall. "I would have liked to have used the long decorator's scissors," thought the old man. "But what is the use of thinking of what I do not have. I must think only of what there is." The length of paper was longer than the pasting table and the old man tied a piece of string across the legs at one end of the table and passed the end of the paper under the string to hold it in place. "I am an old man," he thought, "but I have many tricks, and I have resolution."

He had mixed his paste long before, now the old man lifted the damp cloth that covered the bucket to keep the paste from drying and began to brush the paste on to the paper. He pulled the paper level to the near edge of the table as he pasted the near edge of the wallpaper and pushed it back to the far edge as he pasted the far edge of the paper, and in this way the table stayed clean.

Now he took two corners of the paper between thumb and forefinger and folded almost two feet of the paper back on itself, keeping paste against paste, pattern against pattern, until he had made a concertina of the whole pasted length of paper. He kept the folds loose so as not to crease the paper and he felt the slime-like glue slide between his fingers. He knew if he did not make the concertina, the tension on the paper would be too great and the paper would break, and he would be left holding only the two corners, like the ears of the bull he had once seen killed when he was a young man. Or worse, the paper might tear in the middle where he could not hide the join. He climbed again the steps of the ladder to offer the pasted banner to the wall. "Will the first piece stick well?" he wondered aloud. "If the first piece sticks well I will say five Hail Marys. There, it is said." The old man had no radio and often talked to himself as he worked. He pressed the paper to the wall so that its top edge was an inch higher than the wall and touched against the ceiling. "*Puta de techo*," he said, "I cannot trust you," and he thought how the ceiling did not run true and how many times he had been betrayed by the ceiling. He was wise to have used the plumb line. Then he placed the edge of the paper against the line he had drawn on the wall. The paper slid into place and the old man took the wallpaper brush from his pocket and stroked its bristles across the surface of the paper. He saw the air bubbles beneath the surface and he brushed them out from the paper until the whole drop hung as smoothly as the wall allowed. Then, high up, he tapped the bristles of the brush along the angle where the wall met the ceiling and ran the back of his knife along the recess. When he pulled the paper away from the wall again he could see the crease in the paper. "If I had the scissors it would have been easy to cut along the fold, but you haven't got the scissors," he thought. "You have only the knife and the brush, and that is enough." With the knife he cut away the narrow strip of paper that was not needed. He wiped the knife on his trousers and then threw the strip of paper over the side of the ladder, watching as it dropped to the floor below.

The old man had worked for two days and two nights to strip the old paper and three times he had had to stop to pull nails from the wall and to fill the holes left behind. Once the head of a nail grazed his brow and drew blood. Now on the third day his back ached and his legs were weak. As he stepped down from the ladder, he sank to his knees and again tapped with the brush along the join where the wall met the skirting board, and with the knife he cut away the narrow strip of paper that was left over and tossed it aside. Raising himself, he saw the paper hanging there on the wall, and how beautiful were its bands of colour against the plaster. Then he shouldered the stepladder and carried its weight the short distance to the place where the next length of paper was to be hung.

"If the boy were here he could have the next length pasted and ready," he thought aloud. "A man should not work alone." His legs and shoulders were stiff, and the pasting brush dug into the wounds in his hands. And he felt then the depth of his tiredness and the pain of life.

The old man cut the second drop longer to allow him to match the pattern. Once it was against the wall, he slid the paper until it covered the mark he had drawn on the wall so that the two edges touched each other and then he saw how the pattern continued unbroken across the two lengths of paper. The old man felt good now. He no longer thought of the pain in his hands and in his back, and he no longer thought of the treachery of the ceiling, for it was not the ceiling's fault. He thought of the beauty of the coloured paper that covered the cracks and the discoloured plaster of the wall, and he knew that the paper was his friend. "Be calm and strong old man," he said. "Wall, I respect you very much, but I will paper you before this day is over."

Bleeding a Radiator

with Emily Brontë

TOOLS:
Radiator key

A chill passed over me as the housekeeper led me into the sparsely furnished chamber. Such a dismal atmosphere lay within its walls that were it not for the little window through which the flurries of snow could be seen in all their icy fury, I might have supposed myself in a tomb.

"The master suffers no one to lodge here, so make no noise, and keep your candle away from the door, though you needn't worry about light at the window; he'll not go abroad this night."

I thanked the good soul, the only glimmer of kindness in the hostile gloom that obtained beneath those rafters, and bade her goodnight. I shivered still with the cold and, regretting having left the glow of the fire too soon, I lay down in the little bed and waited for the warmth to return to my limbs. Instead, I felt the cold pinch my nose and the draughts blow down about my cheeks. Looking for their source, I noted a small radiator mounted on the wall beneath the window. Benumbed to my very heart, I quit my covers and approached the device in the hope of eliciting more warmth from the radiator than I had succeeded in drawing from its owner. My fingers tingled at its touch when I found it to be as cold as a headstone and I cursed the inhospitality of the inmates.

The cold blast skirmished around my ankles, no less fiercely than Throttler, the diabolic hound that had given me such a violent welcome on my arrival and who was as much the cause of my confinement here as the snowstorm that now raged outside. Like a mourner by the graveside I stooped down in my borrowed nightshirt and ran my hand along the pipes that led to and from the radiator. I rejoiced to feel the warmth that confirmed the presence of hot water in the pipes and knew that I had only to open the valve for the liquid to fill the iron structure and to begin warming this room that had stood cold for I knew not how long.

Outside the storm had increased in violence and the branches of the fir tree now set up a violent tapping at the window. Shivering, I grasped the grey knob to the left of the headstone and, not without effort, turned it counterclockwise. Scarcely had I begun opening the valve than there came an infernal knocking from beneath the floorboards, as though a host of demons were come to drag the residents of the Heights down to eternal fires. I believe I would have gladly gone with them, in the hope of warmer lodging than I had found here under Mr Heathcliff's roof.

Not wishing the housekeeper to be punished for her charity, I closed the valve and heard the violent knocking subside.

Though she had, indeed, asked me to keep my lodging in this room a secret, she could hardly have intended for me to freeze to death in its keeping, and deciding that my host and his satellites were long overdue a lesson in hospitality, I reopened the valve and heard the pipes renew their fiendish lament, as though all the dead of the moor were beating on the lids of their coffins in demand of freedom, outdoing even the howling of the wind and the tapping of the fir trees.

The drumless tattoo notwithstanding, I now felt some warmth dispersing through the white ironwork, as if a genie had been released from its lamp, though such warmth as there was failed to spread, held back, I surmised, by the presence of air trapped in the system. I cursed myself for setting out on the moor without a radiator key in my pocket, and resolved that since I could no longer hope to keep secret my occupancy of the chamber, I might as well descend to the kitchen, where I hoped to find the necessary tool in the confines of a vast oak dresser. I took up my candle and walked out into the corridor, taking care to close the door as I left.

The orchestra that was making such a noise in my room now found its accompaniment in the quarters below. Where earlier I had left my hosts sitting in silence, staring like automatons into the flames, I was now witness involuntarily to a scene of such unspeakable frenzy that I pinched myself and rubbed my eyes from disbelief. Joseph, his face blackened with ash, was fallen to his knees, beating himself about the face and head, while his master, like the devil himself emerging from the coals, stood before the fire, his arms aloft, his chest bared, howling like a wolf beneath a full moon, "Cathy, my Cathy, I hear you knocking. She is there, Joseph, she is come back."

The dogs joined briefly in the baying of this mad pack, until silenced with a kick by their master as he headed for the stair-well where I now stood in my nightshirt. That old Pharisee, Joseph, followed, his hands clasped about his Bible like a miser's round his purse, as he called aloud to all the saints his credentials as a God-fearing Christian. Trembling, for cold, in all my limbs, I expected no exchange of civilities as they passed and none came. The two brutes scarce gave me a glance as they hurried by, as though summoned to the final judgement. Within moments all previous scenes of madness were forgot-ten. My demonic host flung open the door I had just closed and, in an uncontrollable passion of tears, began calling to every corner of that chamber for his Cathy. "See, she is here, she knocks. Come in, Cathy. Oh, Cathy, forgive me and come home."

I could no more dream of stepping back into that room had the house been in flames, than I could think of intruding on such a gush of grief and superstition. Profiting from the commotion, I continued downstairs where the kitchen of Wuthering Heights was bathed in an eerie red glow. A fine red fire illumined the chimney, and the cur, Throttler, and an Irish terrier called Djinn, accustomed to the ravings of their master, were curled up asleep on the flagstones, confirming that even the dogs of the house were not kept as short of warmth as its guests. Immediately I began to search the drawers of the old dresser, making as little noise as possible. A cold draught now reached down also into the penetralium and I guessed that Mr Heathcliff had thrown wide the window of my chamber and was calling his plea to the storm. "Cathy, come back, my love, my Cathy." Hurrying my search, I pulled open a drawer full of knives and mixing spoons. Rattling through its contents I came upon the object of my search, a small brass T-shaped key that sat shining in the cup of a serving spoon. No sooner was it in my hand than the hair rose on my neck and I froze. Behind me I heard the deep, loathsome rattle of Throttler's growl. Like a sound rising from the Underworld, its profound baritone might have made the room shake if my legs did not already shake so from the cold. The beast had me backed against the dresser and, not for the first time, I was beginning to regret crossing these wretched moors to further the acquaintance of my landlord. As the hairy monster began to pull on my nightshirt, shaking his head as though in violent disagreement at my presence, I saw in the shadows the mistress of the house, watching my discomfort as motionless and mute as had she been contemplating a kitten toying with a mouse. "Madam, I should be glad if you would call your dog off." At a gesture from her slender hand and a sharp call, the little terrier leapt up from the hearth and trotted over to rest his head on his mistress's knee. "I meant rather the dog who has hold of my nightshirt," I hastened to add.

"That. That is not *my* dog," she observed scornfully, caressing the little tawny head and looking for all the world as though the madness that currently held dominion over the household were an everyday amusement. "Were you looking for a knife?" she asked with a note of hope in her voice.

"I was looking rather for a key ..." I struggled to remain on my feet.

"To his room? Have you come to kill him?"

Horrified, I assured the lady of the house that I had no such notion.

"You would have more chance with a knife."

I looked and saw that my hand still clutched a large wooden serving spoon, but before I could better explain my presence in the kitchen, a great bellow came from the upper regions of the house and distracted him of the tireless jaws, so that the creature momentarily loosened its grip on my borrowed nightshirt. Sensing the time had come to make my escape, with a cry of "Fetch", I threw the spoon into the shadows, tore myself free and ran. Mounting the stairs two at a time, I rushed headlong into the little chamber in which Mrs Dean had earlier wished me a pleasant night's rest. Such a sorrowful sight now met my eyes that, extraordinary to report, I forgot my pursuers and stopped still in my tracks. Mr Heathcliff, in an uncontrollable passion of tears, was kneeling beside the bed, from which I had so lately risen. "Look. Look. Her little body has lain here. Oh, see how she has turned down the counterpane." He was holding the pillow to his cheek, soaking it with his tears, "Hear me this time. Oh, Catherine, let me touch your hand. Lay down your blessed cheek once more on this pillow, that I might look upon you. Oh, my darling."

Beneath the window Joseph cited from the scriptures, calling heaven and all its angels to protect him from demons and witches, and to strike down evil-doers.

My indecorous arrival into this strange sermon had a dramatic effect. Eyes wide, the two men looked up, their gaze at first coming to rest on the great rip that scarred my nightshirt. Mr Heathcliff, seeing my eyes move, with a look of guilty authorship, from the pillow he held pressed to his cheek, to the turned-down bed and hollowed mattress, saw immediately his error. All this must have passed in the blink of an eye, for all at once I fell to the floor. With all his weight, Throttler had struck me in the back and now, his great forepaws planted in my shoulder blades, his abominable snorting ringing in my ears, he took up guard, pinning me to the floor. Unmindful of all this, his master rose to his feet, let fall his arm to his side and dropped the white tear-stained pillow to the floor. That old zealot Joseph closed his Bible and made to stand, his brow corrugating in disapproval, as he leant his hand against the radiator.

The two men seemed unmindful of the snarls and barks with which the hounds kept me in such an embarrassing and disagreeable position and they now made to leave the room, stepping over me, as though I were no more than a tussock on the moor. As he passed, Joseph thrust out his evil tongue in expression of his peevish displeasure. "The Lord help us! It's bonny behaviour, sneaking around o't neeght, heating the place like a furnace and making paupers of us all." More of his sermon I could not distinguish, but, had I not been held fast, I believe I would have kicked the aged rascal out of the door. I hemmed and called after my surly host, "Mr Heathcliff. The dogs. If you please."

He looked back and seemed to see for the first time the hound whose huge purple tongue hung slavering on my shoulders as his fangs clasped the wooden mixing spoon. "How dare you. Under my own roof. God confound you, Mr Lockwood. They won't meddle with persons who touch nothing. Throttler, Djinn, come away!"

I felt the four-footed fiend step from my back and, hearing the sound of the dogs' paws following the two men down the staircase, I struggled to my feet. The events of the evening had gone some way to warming me, but still too cold to sleep, I drew near the radiator. Though the lower portion was now quite hot, its upper reaches remained as cold as before, confirming my earlier supposition that there was indeed air in the system. I had not let go of the key in the pursuit and I now put it to good use, loosening the little square valve that protruded like a bolt from the upper corner of the radiator. Scarcely had I given it a half-turn than I heard the rushing sound of escaping air. I remained in that attitude for nearly a minute, waiting for the first sounds of water bubbling as it reached the valve, whereupon I tightened it at once. The transformation was almost immediate. The whole device now seemed to glow with a benign and agreeable warmth, so that I retired not just then, but gathered my pillow from the floor and drew myself upon a chair to better feel its benefit. So I nodded drowsily, contemplating the ghost of my predecessor and wishing for her as sound a sleep as I now hoped for myself, while thawing my legs on what might well have been the first warmth felt in that room for nearly twenty years.

Reglazing a Window

with Milan Kundera

TOOLS:
Hammer
Putty knife
Tape measure

MATERIALS:
Glass cut to fit
Putty
Panel pins

All governments oppose transparency. They oppose it because they know that with transparency comes fragility. Such is the nature of glass. Windows can certainly be made from materials more flexible or less brittle than glass, but what is required more than anything of a window is that it is transparent. All other qualities become secondary, from which Tomas deduced that transparency creates fragility.

The crack in the pane seemed to Tomas the first sign that

the fortress he had so lovingly constructed was no longer impregnable. All his adult life he had maintained between himself and the outside world an invisible barrier through which no one was allowed to pass. When he believed that he could keep her at a distance like all the others, Odile had found a way through, and the broken window proved finally that Tomas had been deceiving himself.

Before their first night together she had called to say she was staying at a hotel nearby. She was wet through when she arrived at his apartment; the city was in the grip of a storm and her eyes looked out through the long hair plastered to her flushed cheeks, like a child's from the bulrushes. Her cheek and chin were bleeding as she stood in the doorway; breathless, she described how in trying to outrun the storm her heels had slipped on the cobbles. He cleaned her wounds, found her fresh clothes to wear and wrapped her hair in a towel, while she stared at him with eyes of love that he mistook for madness. In the morning he collected her bag from the station; there had been no hotel.

The rules of Tomas's fortress did not allow a woman to stay overnight, but the doelike creature that had come to him, wounded in the storm, crossed his drawbridge unchallenged. Five days later the guards awoke to the danger. An old girlfriend was leaving the city, so Tomas took possession of her flat in the building opposite his own and installed Odile there. Now, seven months later, he stood in the little apartment and surveyed the scene. In the lounge every windowpane bar one was cracked, as if fractured by the vibration of Russian tanks entering the city through the streets below. In the bedroom every pane bar one was intact, this last cracked as though a single white dove, thrown off course in a storm, had flown into the building. He knew then that she had been spying on him.

Sitting on the mattress that served Odile as a bed on the nights he did not permit her to sleep with him, Tomas contemplated the broken pane. In places the putty, grown old and brittle, had fallen away and he could see that the nails that had first been used to hold the pane in place had now rusted. He opened the French windows that overlooked the courtyard to remove the broken fragments that lay in the little recess below the window, and it was then, looking back into the apartment, that he saw Odile's camera, set on its tripod, like an invitation awaiting a guest. When finally Tomas gathered his courage to look through the eyepiece he discovered that the double fracture was aligned like the cross hairs of a rifle sight on his own apartment. Of the unlit interior only the area closest to the window was visible and Tomas searched his memory for any incident involving any other of his mistresses that might have been witnessed by Odile. In the lounge the same sequence was repeated: a low three-legged stool was so positioned that looking through the single unbroken pane from such an oblique angle his gaze was directed once more on to the window of his own apartment. And in that moment he recalled Tereza, cross-legged in only her panties as she sat on the chopping block by the kitchen window. She had lingered in the window, describing to him the brightness of the constellation of the Plough in the night sky, and Tomas, remarking that it was the constellation most favoured by Goethe's hero Werther, had then his first presentiment that something awful was about to happen.

Odile had left the apartment early that morning. She knew exactly what she must do. She took great care as she passed the

118

glazier's shop in case she should meet Tomas. She had been precise about what time she wished him to arrive at her apartment. But Tomas was rarely on time and she did not want to look into his eyes and feel her resolve evaporate, so she hurried, her elegant legs dancing and leaping across the paving slabs so lightly that she seemed carried on the morning breeze. In the café a young man rose from his table to greet her, his eyes aflame, as his hungry lips and eyes fell on the offered cheek and downturned lids of the woman before him.

Tomas handed the piece of paper to the glazier. He had measured exactly the recess of each broken pane and told the glazier to reduce the size sufficiently so that the glass would fit easily. The glazier held the small shard that Tomas had brought with him and chose glass of the same weight and thickness. While Tomas searched for putty, pins and a putty knife he listened to the glass cutter's blade as it screeched across the slippery surface. Each traverse ended with the loud crack of ice breaking under heavy feet. Holding the fragile panes, wrapped in newspaper, under his arm, Tomas returned to Odile's studio.

The last debris brushed from the frame, Tomas put in the first pane of glass. It sat comfortably in its new place and he inserted one of the small nails into the top of the frame and tapped it gently with the hammer until it seemed it would stop the pane from falling. He put two more pins along each side of the pane and a final one against its lowest edge. His anxiety for the absent Odile had not completely subsided. For her every moment spent away from Tomas was time lost and he wondered again at the strange alignment of chair, pane and the window of his apartment, and breathed in the heavy linseed scent of the freshly opened putty. He felt the oiliness on his fingers and the rubbery fleshlike consistency of the clay. He tore off a lump between forefinger and thumb, and began to knead and shape it. He thought of Odile, that simple faunlike creature who had arrived from the provinces clinging to the only book she owned. How confident she now was. He had found her the job in the bookshop, introduced her to the theatre, to concerts, to his friends (not all). How much he had taught her, how much he had shaped her. The pane moved and he hammered in another nail to make clear what the balance of power was between them. Then he pressed a lump of the putty into the edge of the windowpane, pressing it firmly into contact with the glass and the wood, and continued to do so with little balls of the putty no more than the thickness of his thumb, overlapping each over the next to ensure a waterproof seal all round the window. Then he sat back down in Odile's chair and looked out across the courtyard. A movement in the window of his own apartment caught his eye. Hurriedly his eye sought for the eyepiece of Odile's camera and, as his greasy fingers fumbled to adjust the focus, his stomach began to rumble. A ray of sunlight bouncing off a window somewhere was illuminating the kitchen and there, her back against the window, he saw the long dark hair of Odile. Dressed only in her underwear she was perched by the kitchen window, on the old butcher's block that served as a work surface. Tomas's stomach rumbled again; his fingers, held so close to his face, filled his nose with the smell of the window putty. He watched the spectacle with the silent concentration that few professors ever see on the face of a student. Then Odile slowly turned her face towards him. Whether she could see him watching he did not know, but he knew this spectacle was intended for him. There was no sign of triumph on her face, nor of love, nor was it the look of hope and desire that he saw whenever he made love to her, but the look of a member of the Greek chorus who seeks to bear witness. Then the fingers of a man's hand pulled her face away and he saw that she was not alone.

When Pushkin accused Georges d'Anthes of being the lover of his wife, the two men fought a duel. Tomas, feeling for the first time since his childhood the pangs of jealousy, lunged forward to snatch up the putty knife, but Tomas's passion was not Pushkin's, so he began to cut and shape the putty round the pane, all the while trying not to think of Odile at the window. The cracked pane had been replaced, but the blow dealt by Odile had fractured more than just a pane of glass, the crack extended way beyond the confines of the window frame, an expanding fault line sapping power throughout his whole world.

Replacing a Light Switch

with Elfriede Jelinek

TOOLS:
Screwdriver

MATERIALS:
Light switch fascia

Electricians are expensive, says Mother. They will take our money to stand around drinking tea. All tradesmen are wolves and women are their natural prey. They will arrive, still picking the remains of their last victim from their teeth. The tradesman, pulling his lips back to bare his fangs, will make a sucking noise. The job is not so simple, a call will have to be made, materials must be bought. Who did this? The work of the last tradesman must be put right. Have you been having a go yourself? It's a total abortion. But he can put it right; at a price.

Mother and child would have to let a cuckoo into their nest, a man who will look over the goods on offer as though *he* is the buyer. Mother would need Rosa's sharp eyes to watch the tradesman's quick hands, to check that he does the work for which he is paid, to see that he is not undoing good work to put it right again, at a price. But the mother pig does not want to let in a wolf when her little piglet is at home. Mother is only an old woman, her sight is weak from watching over her little one. Tradesmen have quick eyes, their gaze falls like fingers, touching everything, evaluating what the two women have to give. Is that an antique chest? It must be worth a few bob. A nice part of town, not cheap around here. Eyes like hands poring over the inventory: crockery and cushions, paintings and silver plate, breasts and buttocks. A tradesman will ask to use the lavatory, prying to see what underwear hangs over the bath; this way he can take stock. What kind of goods are stored in the apartment? Young ones? Old ones? Young ones are best. Some little pigs even wear underwear that says eat me up.

Rosa is perfectly suited to this kind of electrical work, her dexterous fingers fit in small spaces, her sharp eyes are used to looking at lines and symbols, clefs and crotchets. She will never have to do this work in their new flat, there everything will be new, perfect. But this old place is rotting like a corpse, they can't be wasting money on it now. Rosa gives her money to her mother, that way it can be kept safe with their savings. Mother will look after it, for now Rosa needs only a few pennies, for the bus and the tram. It is foolish to give away their hard-earned money, Mother's money, Rosa's earnings, for a simple job they can do themselves. Rosa will do the job, Mother will tell her how.

Has she turned off the power? Mother asks again and again. Her Rosa is precious and must be kept safe, so that one day, if she is not handled roughly, she may become an antique, priceless and pristine because her drawers have never been opened. Has she removed the fuse? Has she turned off the switch?

Rosa undoes the screws on the faceplate of the switch; there are two of them. The new faceplate must be the same size, otherwise they will have to replace the existing box and then she will have to return to the electrical shop to queue among the leering men, to have them brush against her in the queue, to smell their beery, sweaty smell, to be called their darling when she is no one's darling, except Mother's.

Don't lose the screws, says Mother, they will fit back in the same holes. Mother is anxious about fitting screws in holes, she fitted a screw in a hole once and now she has Rosa, and look how much extra work that created for Mother. Years and years to put things right, now they are happy. She sent the tradesman who did that job away. He expected more than a cup of tea. Now he is discarded and Rosa remains the only evidence of his work, but not really, says Mother, any tradesman could have done the same, it is all Mother's work, his part was nothing, a clumsy blow from a hammer, a turn of the screw, a whirr of the power tool, and then he was gone.

Rosa lifts the faceplate away from the box, but strong wires hold the two together. Black and red, yellow and green. Live, neutral, earth, Earth, mother, child. Live and neutral are held together in the same sheath, they are always together, like mother and child. Mother is live, Rosa is neutral. But really Mother is the switch; she tells Rosa when to come on when to go off. Rosa is like a current that Mother controls, for her own safety, for Mother's safety. The fascia panel hangs from the cable like a child hanging from the umbilical cord; it can never be cut or the child will die, the mother will die. One after the other Rosa loosens the screws and pulls the wires free; now she can discard the old cracked control; disconnected it is useless.

The switch is serviced by a two-core and earth cable. The wires are all cocooned together in the plastic sheath. The earth conductor is still connected to the terminal at the back of the mounting box. The red and black conductors must be connected to the new switch. That's what Mother demands. You strip the wire, then you push it into the hole, where you screw it up tight so the wire cannot escape and other wires cannot enter. The back of the faceplate is marked top so that you cannot put it on upside down. This way the switch is down when the light is on and up when the light is off. It could work just as well upside down but that is not how things are done. This way Mother can always tell if the light is on or off. Rosa would like to put it on upside down, but Mother won't allow it. Use sticky tape to mark which wire goes where, snaps Mother, but there are only two wires, and they can be connected to any terminal. If there were more, Rosa could have disconnected them one at a time or marked them with labels, but that is not necessary.

Rosa removes the little screws, like grubs dormant in their holes, and pulls the wires loose. Mother is anxious; as long as the wires hang loose she is worried for her little treasure; she does not want to see her treasure electrocuted. Rosa inserts the wires into the terminals of the new faceplate and returns the screws. The holes won't be open for long, soon they will all be shut up tight, like Mother's and Rosa's, that way nothing can get in and make sparks. A short circuit would mean that Mother would no longer control the switch and that would be dangerous.

Replacing a Light Switch

Rosa screws the faceplate back in place. Its single ivory key awaits a virtuoso's touch, not a heavy hand. No man will flick this switch. Rosa replaces the fuse and switches the power back on. See, there was no need to let a man into the house to prod clumsily at their switch with his dangerous tool. Now brave Mother can be the first to test the switch. When her finger touches the key the light goes on, and when she presses it again the light goes off. That is how she likes it.

Painting a Room

with Haruki Murakami

TOOLS:
5" emulsion brush
Emulsion roller (optional)
2" gloss brush
Filler knife

MATERIALS:
2.5 litres white emulsion
5 litres blue emulsion
2 litres white gloss
Sugar soap
Sandpaper
Filler

I was twenty-three when I fell in love for the first time, a love that nearly killed me, like a volcano that draws villagers near to its fertile slopes, then covers them with ash, preserving them in a kind of frozen animation for thousands of years, except I survived to tell the tale and my internment didn't last a thousand years, not quite.

I had just graduated from the Kobe School of Journalism when I moved to Tokyo. I knew a few people there but the first friend I made in the new city was Aoko. She occasionally worked as a hostess in a well-known jazz club in the Shinjuku district. I would go there and make a whisky last all night, avoiding talking to anyone and losing myself in the music. When one day I recognised her shopping in a record store, I invited her for coffee. Over time it became a regular event and gradually she told me about herself, how her boyfriend, Toru, had killed himself the year before in his car; how her father had recently passed away after a long illness; how she had once studied the piano but could now no longer bear to touch one. She had just found a new apartment; it was in a run-down part of town but the landlord had offered a great price, as long as Aoko cleaned it up herself.

Aoko – her name meant blue – was wearing a white coat, tied at the waist, her long hair reached almost to the table top, she looked good, even under the fluorescent lighting. I had made money to put myself through college by decorating other people's houses and offered to help. She looked good enough that I would have offered, even if I had never seen a tin of paint. That time she refused, but a few months later, when I saw her again in the jazz club, she asked if the offer was still open. She still looked great and it was.

The boxy room had been given up on so long ago that we couldn't even date the décor. We cleared the room of Aoko's few belongings and together pushed the bed into the middle of the room. Aoko, dressed in a pale blue cotton shirt and cut-off jeans, used masking tape to fix plastic sheets along the skirting boards at the edge of the floor, while I used the heavier cotton dust sheets to cover the furniture in the middle of the room.

The first task was to wash the years of grime from the walls, ceiling and woodwork. I filled a bucket with warm water and sugar soap, and, wearing purple rubber gloves I'd got from a temporary job in a pharmaceutical company, we began washing the room from top to bottom. Old cobwebs and dust were thick in the corners, and we were soon soaked with water and sweat. Judging from the yellow colour of what must have once been white, the previous resident had smoked about a hundred cigarettes a day, but the sugar soap cut through the dirt and grease as the two of us worked our way down from the ceiling to the floor. I looked across at Aoko standing on the steps so she could reach up into the corners, her right arm moving back and forth with the sponge as though she were waving to someone invisible beyond the wall. As her arm moved her body swayed elegantly, her slim hips hugged tightly by her cut-offs. My imagination kicked in and I thought of her body, naked against mine, but that happy outcome, if it was ever to occur, was still some way off in our story. When we had finished with the washing the room looked almost as if it had been repainted already. Who would believe so much stuff could cling to a vertical surface, but two buckets of dark, grimy water showed how much the years had deposited on the walls of this small room.

I had finished my side of the room and left off working. "Hey, Aoko, do you have a telephone? I need to make a call." She called me over to the window and pointed to a call box just below in the street. "What if someone wants to call you?"

129

"I don't give the number out much, but if I'm dressed and ready I can make it to the payphone in fifty-two seconds."

After the call I went for coffee, doughnuts and cigarettes. When I came back Aoko was admiring our work. I handed her a coffee. She said thank you. We sat on the top of our stepladders. Her slim hips, almost prepubescent, fitted comfortably into her lofty seat.

"Stopping for doughnuts and coffee is the best bit," I said. "Admiring your own work while you sit back and relax. At every stage there's something new to admire and enjoy. We'll start filling and sanding next."

"You're amazing, Yuri, I wouldn't have a clue about any of this stuff. I would have just started putting the paint on."

"Well, you could have, most people just want to get to what they think of as the best bit, but on top of all that grime it would soon have started to peel off."

I went into the kitchen to mix some filler. The kitchen was even worse, it smelt of fat and it looked like a murder scene. I poured some of the grey-white powder into a bowl, added water and then mixed until it was like rice porridge. The filler was going to cover all the small cracks and holes that we could find. Over the years so many pictures had been nailed up in the room it looked like a mouldy cheese. I divided the mixture into two lots and with filling knives we started to give the walls back their youth, filling the wrinkles and pockmarks until the wall was peppered with dashes of white filler.

"Hey, Yuri, I'm not sure I've got the hang of this. I can't seem to get a smooth finish with this knife."

"Don't worry," I said. "We'll use sandpaper when it's dry."

As she concentrated on her work Aoko held her tongue in

the corner of her mouth. I watched her, wondering how her tongue would feel on mine. She noticed I'd stopped work and pulled her tongue back into her mouth.

"Hey, I'm going faster than you."

"Not for long," I said, but I couldn't forget that tongue.

By now the ceiling and walls had dried, and we could start to paint the ceiling, brilliant white. Aoko wanted to use the paint roller. "Well, it's faster but it sends little specks of paint everywhere and the colours never look as bright. But go ahead if you want to try it," I said. While Aoko rollered the paint on to the middle of the ceiling I painted the corners and edges with a large brush. Above us the ceiling grew whiter, while the furniture, draped in white sheets, lay like a winter landscape below, and we two hovered in between like winter birds on the wing. When finally I had to descend to change the music, I took off Bill Evans's "Waltz for Debbie" and put on "Kind of Blue". From below I watched Aoko, her movements elegant and economical, her balance perfect at the top of the steps. I looked up in awe.

We knew the ceiling would need two coats but for now we waited for it to dry. Aoko put a Marlboro between her lips and the two of us took a break, the smoke rising in time with the piano towards the white of the ceiling; already its brilliance was under assault. I found a bottle of Courvoisier in the next room and poured two glasses.

"You drink brandy in the morning?" Aoko looked surprised.

"I try not to drink anything stronger before midday."

She laughed. "You're crazy, Yuri." She took the glass and her lips touched its rim with all the impact of a butterfly landing on a flower. I wondered how it would feel to have that butterfly land on my mouth and watched her nose wrinkle as she sniffed the aroma of the cognac.

"You're not trying to get me drunk?" she joked.

"I thought about it." I was honest.

I'd been with a few girls since I'd known Aoko, but it was pointless. Other relationships were like games of Russian roulette. I could sleep with them a few times, if the revolver fired on an empty chamber it was fine, but sooner or later the chamber that contained my feelings for Aoko would click into place and then blam, a bullet to the brain and it was game over.

Once before I had succeeded in getting Aoko drunk. We were sharing a cab on the way home when she forgot herself and kissed me on the mouth, two butterflies collided and finally I understood chaos theory. The resulting tidal wave crashed through my world, sweeping everything away. When the tide fell back it took everything with it and the emergency services couldn't get to me.

I had been watching Aoko for too long now without speaking. She picked up a piece of sandpaper. "Hey, Yuri, how do they make this stuff? Is it really sand?"

"Sure, there are teams working in the Gobi Desert. First with brushes they paint glue on to huge sheets of paper and then gangs of Gobi people lay the paper face down on the sand so that it sticks. If you look carefully, sometimes you can see little pieces of camel shit." Aoko laughed and gave me that cute look that said she couldn't be taken for a fool. The old balance was returned, good old Yuri. "I expect the filler's dry enough now. Let's rub it down, but use the fine paper, we'll use the rough stuff they make in Arizona for the woodwork."

The shooshing sound of sandpaper on plaster filled the room and a fine white powder settled on everything, dusting Aoko's black hair with icing sugar, collecting on eyelashes and lips; we were rapidly ageing together in a room covered with white sheets and it reminded me of a character I had once read about in Dickens. Somehow Aoko looked just as beautiful. Her whitening hair was tied back and she had on a pair of white gym shoes. She had good technique, a light touch that left each area beautifully smooth. While I sanded the door frame, skirting board and windows I watched her through the dust as she reached up to sand a patch that we'd filled high on the wall, her cotton shirt stretched taut over her breast revealing the shape of her nipple. Desire weighed in my trousers like a rock. The urge to take her in my arms was now almost overwhelming and the shooshing had become the sound of my blood rushing in my ears.

I stood behind her, kidding myself that I was looking at the work. You can only kid yourself for so long and I reached out and placed my hand on the back of her neck; her hair felt soft and smooth against my palm.

"That's enough," I said. Aoko froze, facing the wall, her hand still in its raised position; her hips were just a few inches from mine and I could feel the warmth coming from her body. I moved closer, my face level with her perfect ear, the scent of her sweat and perfume mingling with the dust. We stayed like that, immobile, listening to each other's breathing. Now that the sanding had stopped the sound of Coltrane playing "How Deep Is the Ocean" could be heard again. It was deep. I reached my left hand around her body and laid it on her breast.

Aoko was the first to speak. "Yuri san, you are my best friend, but I cannot be your girlfriend." She twisted round to face me, her face bowed; a tear ran down, leaving a glistening trail on the geisha whiteness of her cheek. I said nothing. I felt sick with myself.

"I am sorry, Yuri." Her face was still bowed. "I am not a good person for you. I will make you unhappy and I never want to do that to you. I am not as balanced as I seem and I don't want thoughts of me to hold you back. Find a nice normal girl to be your girlfriend. If you fall in love with me we can no longer be friends."

"I'm not going to kill myself, if that's what you're afraid of." I regretted it as soon as I said it. Outside the rain had begun to fall, and I thought of Toru putting his foot down on the gas and driving himself all the way to the other side, while still in neutral.

"I need to go out. Did you say we need some more gloss paint?"

I needed to go out too and stand in the rain, but Aoko had beaten me to it. "Yeh, one more litre of white gloss for the doors." I didn't try to stop her. The door closed with a click that sounded like the full stop on a vintage typewriter.

I drank another brandy and smoked a cigarette. Had I made a mistake? At the time I thought so, but now, nearly twenty years later, I'm not so sure. It didn't take me long to paint a second coat of emulsion on the ceiling and then I opened the paint for the walls: powder-blue, Aoko had chosen the colour. I stirred the liquid with a stick and then, using the wide emulsion brush, began painting the edges and corners of the room. Concentrating on the brushstrokes cleared my mind. The frame of blue that outlined the room looked so nice I could have left it that way. Aoko was taking a long time, but I guessed she needed some space. I might even have the walls painted by the time she got back. A few hours later the first coat was finished. It looked great. Light patches showed where we had used the filler but they would disappear under the second coat. It was getting late and I stopped for something to eat. I found some noodles and miso soup in the kitchen, and ate looking out of the window at the endless April rain. Where was Aoko? Why was she taking so long? By nightfall I had painted a second coat and finished the brandy. I eventually passed out on Aoko's bed, everything in the room still covered by the white dust sheets.

It was some weeks before I heard from Aoko again. I carried on living in her apartment, even after I had finished all the painting, but I left the sheets over everything, as if she had just left the room. I brought a few things from my own place but I didn't like to leave for long in case she called or showed up. One night I was woken by the sound of the telephone. I knew it was Aoko. I slept in my clothes just in case. Running through the wet street, my breathing fast and tennis shoes sliding, I made it to the receiver before the ringing stopped. On the other end of the line I could hear cars driving through wet streets. No one spoke but I knew it was Aoko. Was she holding the receiver or was it just hanging there picking up the sound of the street? At least it was raining there; we were standing in the same rain. My head leant against the glass as I looked out at the passing headlights. I told her about the apartment and how good the blue looked. "When you get back we can decide where to hang your Blue Note posters." I carried on for a while, telling her all about the room, how I'd washed down the woodwork with white spirit before giving it two coats of gloss, how I'd had to leave the windows open until the paint dried so that they didn't stick shut. I talked on, about the bird that landed on the window ledge and about the cat that came in from the neighbour's apartment. I kept talking, about anything, until the sound of cars passing in the rain at the other end of the line became waves on the beach. Finally I stopped talking, wondering if she was listening, how long the credit would last, but I couldn't let go of the telephone, or stop looking out at the rain and thinking of the endless sea.

Tiling a Bathroom

with Fyodor Dostoevsky

TOOLS:
Hammer
Spirit level
Scraper
Tile cutter
Sponge
Wooden batten
Tape measure
Dust sheet

MATERIALS:
Tiles
Spacers
Tile adhesive
Tile grout

With a sort of stoic resignation Pokoroff rang the doorbell of the apartment on K—— Street. The threadbare bag of tools that he held in his hand now seemed to him pathetically inadequate for one claiming to be a fully served tiler and he hoped the old woman would not notice the deception. His ragged clothes, smeared and shiny with oil, were only to be expected on one about to undertake dirty work and now, down to his last few kopeks, the student was desperate for money. Behind the door, he could hear the old lady's slippered feet shuffling along the hall and, at the sound of a bolt being pulled aside, he tightened his grip on the rough handle and composed himself. Two eyes peered out at him from the interior. "Is that all you have brought?" said their owner distrustfully.

"I have what I need. Could you please show me to the bathroom?" As he spoke he fancied there was a gleam of mockery in the widow's eyes. A musty odour emerged from the old woman's lodgings and Pokoroff pushed past her with the air of one who tries to appear confident, but does so only with great pains.

The heat in the apartment was stifling as she led him through a small parlour. The light here seemed to be of a yellow or rather greenish hue, and Pokoroff's eye was drawn to the mantelpiece, where a collection of holy images competed for space with a group of rustic figures in porcelain, and a bitter smile played about our hero's lips. "Here we are batuchka. My son-in-law has left the materials there under the sink. I will be back around four."

Pokoroff's heart sank as he now contemplated the repulsive character of his surroundings. Above the basin a spotted mirror reflected an ancient tub, itself discoloured by the dirty brown stain that led from dripping tap to plughole. A rickety table, topped with jars of bath salts, separated the bath from the newly disinfected toilet bowl, while between mirror and basin a cracked splashback, missing a brace of tiles, clung precariously to the wall. A sliver of soap and a chipped glass, containing a set of false teeth and a balding toothbrush, completed the inventory.

"Perhaps you could leave me a little money in advance," said our hero, pretending to take stock of the materials left by the son-in-law. In later times Pokoroff would wonder at his own cunning. "It is conceivable that I may need more adhesive or grouting before the day is done."

The old woman took a white leather pouch from her bag and undid its clasp. The greasy purse must have contained over a hundred roubles and, not wishing to arouse suspicion, Pokoroff diverted his gaze to the sinciput of the old lady's head where scant curls failed to conceal her pallid scalp in the greenish light. A sudden pressure in his hand brought him back to himself and with a scornful look he observed the ten-rouble note she had pressed into his palm.

"Is that all?" he exclaimed with excessive irritation.

Perceiving his disappointment the old lady smiled. "Well, let me pay you for your work now, and if you have cause to buy more materials I will refund the difference later." And so saying she counted fifty roubles into our hero's trembling hand. "I'm sure I can trust you to do a good job."

The self-styled tiler crammed the notes into the pocket of his ragged coat and, discerning an interrogatory note in this last statement, knitted his brows as he watched her leave the apartment, closing the door behind her.

For the first time, Pokoroff now opened the bag of tools he had stolen from the tool shed at the back of his lodgings and cast on its aged contents a look of flashing rage. "To think that

I have been such a fool," he muttered. He saw now that the bag contained not the tools of his landlady, but those of her gardener. "This is exactly the sort of trifle that could spoil everything."

Feeling crushed, nay humiliated, he caught up the gardener's sickle and plunged its rusty blade behind the tiles above the sink. Long age and humidity had weakened the glue that held them in place so that they easily came away, crashing into the sink and shattering with a great noise as they did so. Their removal revealed an ugly rectangular patch of ridged and hardened adhesive. Pokoroff scraped now at this in an attempt to render the surface smooth, but the glue, so ineffective at holding the tiles in place, showed more resistance at clinging to the wall. Using a stabbing action the worker saw that little chips of the dried adhesive broke off, occasionally flying up into his face, and in this way he gradually succeeded in levelling the most irregular ridges formed by the glue.

The old woman, as is the way with old women who leave nothing to chance, had left a sack for rubbish and Pokoroff now began filling it with the debris from the sink. The jagged edges of the broken tiles were sharp and when he saw that a crack had appeared on the surface of the basin, he flew into a rage. How could he have been so unthinking? He might easily have placed some covering over the basin to cushion the fall of the tiles. With bitter disgust he saw that he had also managed to cut himself and that blood was dripping from his hand. It had already splashed his shoes and the floor before he thought to hold the wound over the open refuse bag. The thick red liquid dripped onto the broken tiles where the drops stained their white surface red. He grew light-headed and for a moment it seemed to him that the tiles were smiling at this benediction, until he realised that this was no chimera. Half buried in the detritus, the widow's false teeth came as a disagreeable surprise. In his haste he had forgotten to clear the room. "Details, details," he murmured and, looking up, he saw clearly the remains of the glass that had held the teeth mingling with the broken tiles in the sink. Reluctantly he recovered the gory teeth and dropped them out of sight into his pocket. He then wrapped his injured hand with a rag and watched as the white fabric turned red with blood.

Pokoroff felt giddy. Desperate to escape the stifling atmosphere of the apartment, he headed for the back door, which led to a small yard. He stood on the step, breathing deeply and offering up his face to the breeze. As he did so he beheld a line full of laundry, no doubt washed and hung out to dry that very morning while he himself had still been abed, struggling to rise after a night of disturbed and unrefreshing slumber.

He snatched a handkerchief from the line and replaced the bloody rag, which he hung up to dry in its place. Looking about him, he then tore a large sheet free from its pegs and returned to the bathroom, where he used it to protect the fading white enamel of the bathtub. Our worker was in a hurry to be gone and now he did not hesitate. Taking up the sickle he set about him, stabbing frantically at the walls, levering tiles loose in ones and twos, until the walls stood bare and the bath groaned under the weight of the debris.

Burning with impatience he tore open the package of tiles and with a piece of garden twine measured one of the sides. His plan was to attach a batten, procured expressly for the purpose, to the wall at precisely the height of the second row of tiles. This would prevent the tiles sliding down the wall, and ensure that they were level and did not follow the slope of the bath. He placed two of the masonry nails between his lips and took up the batten, but he was now interrupted in his work. Where was the hammer? Spitting out the nails, he searched the bag again, turning it upside down and shaking it until a garden trowel and a hatchet fell onto the bathroom floor. A sickly smile appeared on his lips. Lacking a spirit level, he did his best to confirm the batten was indeed level. There was now not a moment to lose. Brandishing the hatchet, he swung it, almost mechanically, on to the head of the first nail. The sharp fixing penetrated the soft wood. With increasing vigour Pokoroff struck two more blows, driving the nail on into the wall. He checked again the level of the batten, held up a second nail and, with his full strength, drove the nail clear through wood and plaster, pinning the piece of wood in place. It was done. Thick drops of sweat trickled down his neck as he began laying on the tile adhesive, a few feet at a time. His hands shaking, his lips parched, he pressed each tile into place with a kind of monomania. Among the materials left by his employer, Pokoroff found a packet of tiny white plastic crosses and these he used to ensure the tiles were evenly spaced. A desire to escape these scornful lodgings made him desperate. Without a tile cutter he used the garden shears to cut the last pieces for the corners of the room before finally he turned to renew the half-dozen tiles above the handbasin.

How many obstacles, how many tasks yet stood between our hero and his freedom. The wooden batten was still attached to the wall and the grouting required mixing before it could be used to fill the grid of gaps that lay between the tiles. Bracing one foot in the bath, he pulled at the batten, he heaved, but the nail held fast. His impatience was intense as he used the hatchet to lever off the offending article. When finally it gave way, Pokoroff lurched backwards, the hatchet flew from his hand, crossed the narrow width of the room and landed with a crash in the basin. This time a deep jagged crack split the white cranium of the sink from tap to plughole. Pokoroff staggered back in disbelief, prey to sombre thoughts that his way of going to work was probably not the one circumstances demanded. Time was drawing on and the old lady might return at any moment.

From the kitchen he then took a pail, which he filled with grouting powder, adding sufficient water to make a smooth paste, before leaving the compound to stand. Pokoroff then applied the last of the adhesive to the wall where the batten had lately been removed, and fixed the final row of tiles in place. The grouting was now ready, but Pokoroff stood irresolute, until footsteps resounded on the landing. Scarcely daring to breathe, Pokoroff listened. When finally a key was pushed into the lock, the rattling of the handle shook him from his torpor. Pokoroff closed the bathroom door. Frantically he now began to slop grouting into the gaps; one by one the tiny white crosses between the tiles disappeared from sight beneath the grey paste. The mistress of the house could be heard calling aloud, "Batuchka! I am back. I will make some some tea. Will you take a cup?" The grouting done, he took up the damp sponge and began to wipe away the grey paste that splattered tiles, bath, clothing, everything. He was now in full possession of his intellect. Avoiding his reflection as he washed his hands, Pokoroff saw that the sink was shattered. From the cracked basin water spurted out in streams onto the floor. "Do not come in yet," he called aloud, "I have a surprise for you." He then took up the hatchet from the floor and, with a heave, hoisted the four corners of the sheet from the bath and made of it a sackful of broken tiles that he slung over his shoulder.

With a cry of "Close your eyes…" Pokoroff rushed out of the back door of the apartment. Stooping under his load, he passed under the red rag that hung from the line, staggered down the steps into the garden, and swung the sheet and its contents over the fence to land with a crash in the neighbouring yard. He then climbed up onto the garden wall and jumped down into the street.

On landing he fell awkwardly. A sharp pain coursed through his hip, but there was no time to stop. He limped on, trying to merge unseen with the afternoon crowds, to quit the neighbourhood before the widow had time to raise the alarm. He no longer felt shame at being seen in clothes stained by common labour, rather a fierce pride, the pride of one who earns his living by the sweat of his brow and the strength of his limbs, whose wounds are the honours of battle. Tired physically, he saw before him the promise of restful slumber, of the peace afforded to one whose work bears fruit for all, whose efforts bring dignity and salvation.

Suddenly he found himself the subject of catcalls; a drunk swaying on the steps of the dram house drew the attention of passers-by with a shout: "Look at the polka dancer!" He was now mimicking the wayward, loping gait of the injured Pokoroff. He tried to increase his speed, to outpace the tipsy clown, but the pain in his hip grew more acute. Pokoroff turned to confront his accuser. "What are you driving at? I am a worker. You would do well to take note that I have tiled a bathroom today with my own hands!" A busy public thoroughfare was no place to remedy matters and Pokoroff was obliged to stumble on, accompanied by the play-acting of the drunkard, his efforts to outpace him rendered more painful by the pressure of the old woman's false teeth as they bit deep into his thigh.

Putting up a Shelf

with Julius Caesar

TOOLS:
Drill
Screwdriver
Spirit level

MATERIALS:
Wood for shelf
Brackets
Screws
Rawlplugs

The house comprised three areas, the upper floor, dominated by the Adulesceni, the ground floor, under the control of Caesar's wife, and the external land, all under the sole control of Caesar himself. By granting autonomy to the rulers of these other areas Caesar hoped better to keep the peace, but recently Caesar's wife had petitioned him, arguing that her territory was too small. The ground floor was divided into lounge, dining room, study and kitchen, and it was in the area of the kitchen that Caesar's wife complained of insufficient space and work surfaces. Caesar was informed that a large part of the work space was taken up with condiments, appliances and recipe books, and he saw that there was a need for a shelf to relieve congestion.

Caesar's wife is in almost daily conflict with the Adulesceni, either trying to keep them out of her territory or raiding their settlements on the upper floor with the aim of imposing her customs and laws. The Adulesceni are known for their hostility and cruelty, even to their own kind; their territory on the upper floor consisted of two rooms, virtually closed to outsiders. The bathroom, designated as a neutral area open to all, had now also come under their domination.

As a tribe the Adulesceni are exempt from almost all work and do not pay taxes like ordinary citizens. They regard it as their greatest glory to lay waste as much as possible of the land around them so as to make it uninhabitable. The gods they reverence change almost constantly and they decorate their dwellings and clothing with images of the god most in favour. They also worship the Greek god Nike and the old Norse god Nokia, in his ever changing forms. They measure their time not by days but by nights and their belief that the day begins at night is supported by their sleeping for most of the daylight hours. They regard it as unbecoming to be seen in the presence of their parents and those who preserve their chastity least are most highly commended by their friends.

The customs of Caesar's wife are entirely different. The only gods she recognises are things that she can see and by which she is obviously benefited, such as the sun, jewels, fabrics, slaves; the other gods she has never even heard of. Though she talks often of making sacrifices, she and her tribe are not much given to the practice. She is fiercely competitive with others of her kind and they make almost weekly raids on the merchants in search of plunder, which she often presents as a tribute to the Adulesceni. These raids are a constant nuisance to Caesar and the treasury.

For this reason Caesar recognised that he must act soon to remedy her complaints and immediately gave orders for the necessary materials to conduct the campaign. Caesar levied wood for a shelf measuring two metres long, twenty centimetres deep and two and a half centimetres thick, three brackets to be placed at regular intervals, screws and Rawlplugs. He also gathered tools – a drill with number eight masonry bit, a screwdriver and a spirit level.

Caesar chose to locate the shelf directly above the work surface but within reach of Caesar's wife. Above the worktop was situated a light switch. Caesar had been informed that concealed wiring extended above this switch in a direct line vertically. Caesar wanted to avoid locating the brackets along this axis and positioned the shelf accordingly.

But before his arrangements were completed a deputation arrived from the Adulesceni to complain that the curfew set in the district kept them from proper worship of their gods and was causing them to lose face before other members of their tribe. In addition there was to be a gathering of their people which, if they were unable to attend, would damage their standing immeasurably.

When Caesar reminded them of their responsibilities to

their mother, who had extended her protection, and in calling them children recalled their failure to observe the rules of the home by the recent smuggling of banned substances into Caesar's own quarters, they prostrated themselves before him with tears in their eyes. Caesar reminded them of the important privileges conferred upon them by himself and by his wife. Caesar answered the deputation that he would consider the matter, but now insisted that they leave with him a hostage who would serve in the current undertaking. The deputation, on hearing of Caesar's request, hung their heads in dejection, their eyes fixed upon the ground, such is the Adulesceni's hatred of work. In astonishment Caesar reminded them of the consequences if they failed to pay tribute to him, so Caesar prevailed.

Thus, while the hostage held the shelf in position Caesar took the spirit level and, placing it on the wooden surface, made adjustment so that the shelf was horizontal. Fearing that the hostage could not be trusted to hold the length of wood steady for long, Caesar drew a line in pencil under the shelf. Caesar then took the first bracket and positioned it towards one end of the line, taking care to keep the bracket both vertical and level with the underside of the shelf. Caesar then marked the three holes of the bracket on the wall and took up his drill with the number eight masonry bit. He drilled the first hole and filled it with a Rawlplug. When Caesar saw that the hole was so deep that the Rawlplug was now out of reach of the screw, he wrapped a piece of tape round the drill bit, one Rawlplug's length from its point. The next two holes went according to plan and Caesar was able to screw the first bracket into place.

Now when he saw Caesar's full attention on the task in hand, the hostage broke ranks and made his escape. Know that all men naturally love freedom and hate servitude; the Adulesceni moreover are fond of idleness and angry to be brought from their settlements in daylight. Engaged as he was in operations on the east wall, Caesar was unable to fight on two fronts and could not put down the rebellion straight away. Caesar decided to allow the hostage to leave, but not to let the rebellion go unpunished in case the Adulesceni should despise him for weakness.

The drilling for the second bracket showed the wall in this section to be of plasterboard and not of brick. When the first Rawlplug was lost in the action, falling into the cavity behind the wall, Caesar saw that his labour was being wasted. One device that Caesar had procured proved useful, special Rawlplugs made for plasterboard. These were more conical in shape and, when tightened with a screw, opened to better grip the plasterboard. With their aid the work was now a common task to which Caesar easily proved superior. The brackets fixed, Caesar put the shelf in place. One hour after collection of the timber had begun the work was completed. On the conclusion of the shelving campaign Caesar's wife came to offer congratulations with promises of peace and friendship, which Caesar graciously accepted. Caesar quartered his tools and marched on the Adulesceni stronghold where a grim struggle was anticipated. The speed of his advance, however, threw them into a sudden panic and Caesar, spurred on by the recollection of their earlier treachery, burst into their camp and, in a demonstration of strength, seized their god Ipod.

Caesar had achieved all the objects for which he had laboured, to overawe Caesar's wife, punish the Adulesceni and to relieve the kitchen of pressure on space. In this short period Caesar considered he had done all that honour or interest required.

Repairing a Dripping Tap

with Marguerite Duras

TOOLS:
Spanner

MATERIALS:
Washer

The man passes for a second time in front of the house and stops. He rings the doorbell. The door is open, he enters. The interior is light, furnished in white. A woman's voice:

"So you've come."

She is standing. She watches. She watches a sink, a tap. He advances towards her. She sees him come. His clothes are dark. His eyes bright. She smiles. He takes one more step, he stops beside her. With a mechanical gesture she shows the tap. From the tap, drips of water fall into the sink. The tap is watched.

The light fades.

Man, woman, tap. He moves, he opens the tap. The noise of water growing louder, the falling water thunders, shattering white in the sink to disappear into the abyss, to join other tributaries, and channels forming a great mass of water, going down to the sea. To the caverns of the sea. He closes the tap. The noise subsides. Silence. The silence is broken by the dripping of the tap.

"I think the washer's gone."

She speaks. Her tone requires no reply.

"The washer's gone."

He replies.
Drips fall one by one. Drops of water that refuse to wait in the darkness of the pipe for permission to run.

"He does it up too tight. He doesn't like the tap to drip," she says.

The man bends to turn off the water supply. Then he straightens, he opens the tap fully. Briefly the noise of running water returns. Suddenly the water stops. The dripping stops. Silence. Outside, beyond the terrace, dusk descends on the town. The light runs out of the sky, draining into the west. Now, in the silence, the sound of the sea reaches into the kitchen. The sea, formless, uncontained, untapped, beyond compare. A scream cries out, like the sound of a woman falling.

*

"What was that?" he asks

"What?" She lifts her face slightly. He is not looking at her.

"That cry."

"Nothing. The sound of the gulls."

The story begins.

Between the man and the window the woman is walking; her hand raised like a child's, she covers her eyes. The floorboards creak beneath her feet. In front of him the tap. He rests his hand on the shiny metal. He sees the capstan head, beneath the head the shroud covers the gland nut, the spindle, the headgear nut, the jumper. Beneath the jumper, out of sight, the flattened washer, compressed, decomposed, destroyed.

The man unscrews the metal shroud to reveal a large nut just above the body of the tap. With a spanner he unfastens the nut, he removes the headgear of the tap. He detaches the streaming mechanism, he offers it to her. The light dances in his eyes.

"The washer's gone."

They look, they look at each other, they wait.

He repeats,

"The washer's gone. Look, look here, look."

He shows her the washer, laid waste, the ravages of time, the build-up of limescale, the pressure created by the ever tightening tap, fighting to hold back the flow, the tide. The brutal accumulation of force.

She says she understands. She makes an effort not to cry.

With a screwdriver he prises off the old washer, cracked, wrinkled, prematurely aged. He takes a new one from his tool-box. The new washer sits pertly in his hand, smooth, firm, thick as cream on milk. It slips tightly over the little button on the jumper at the base of the headgear. He replaces the mechanism into the tap, screwing it tightly back into place, he lowers the shroud, the shiny cover that hides the tap's mechanism beneath a coat of gleaming metal, he bends down, he opens the mains valve. The last of the light drains from the sky, in the darkness they hear the water forced back into the pipe, hear the pressure rise beneath the washer. He straightens, opens the tap, he closes the tap. They watch. They wait. Nothing drips. Nothing flows. Everything is stopped, everything is held back.

He returns his spanner to the toolbox. He looks at her.

"You're crying."
"I'm crying?"

Silence.

She is standing next to him, but her eyes look into the distance, at the last fiery clouds as they slip one by one over the horizon.

Boarding an Attic

with Edgar Allan Poe

TOOLS:
Claw hammer
Ripsaw

MATERIALS:
Floor-grade chipboard
Nails
Wood adhesive

The long and weird catalogue of human misery has its own dark hierarchy. Accounts of flood and famine, plague and pestilence, earthquake and eruption rightfully thrill us and command the attention of our most august journals, the sympathy of our governments and the generosity of our charitable societies. Yet can the misery of the individual who shares his fate with friend and neighbour, citizen and countryman, neath the ineluctable and unforeseeable wrath of whatever Authority he chooses to honour, bear comparison with the true wretchedness and ultimate woe of one who suffers in the knowledge that he alone has cultivated the seeds of his own destruction? The good husband, who sought to surprise his spouse with a new electrical light fitting, awaited her return in smouldering convulsions, his deadly caress an extension of the galvanic wire. The Sunday arborist who fell from his ladder, still clutching the hired chainsaw, no more merciful than Death's scythe, to harvest the soul of his wife, deadheading roses below him. Such handymen have truly walked the shores of the Ultima Thule of torment.

Over long years I had amassed a vast collection of papers relating to these and other such incidents. Books, journals, newspaper cuttings, actuarial reports and more, all gathered in the course of my profession, accumulated in my study and beyond, until there was scarce space to admit the rare visitor who still troubled to call on me. Eventually that rare caller, my friend and physician, Doctor Garrett, prevailed upon me to create a separate storehouse for my collection and so liberate the living quarters of my residence from a burden that threatened to engulf them completely. So did I find myself in the cathedral-like structure of commingled gloom and grandeur that occupied the uncharted peaks of the ancient and dilapidated property wherein I had made my home. My intention was to lay a floor. To this end I had made measurements and caused to be delivered a quantity of floor-grade chipboard of the tongue-and-groove variety. Working from the corner furthest from the feeble light source, which scarce illumined my labours, I began to lay the boards. Those dark recesses, unlooked upon since that cloak of slate first enveloped them in eternal night, resisted my intrusion like the densest thicket. Lost in a forest of strut and rafter, hangar and purlin, my feet stumbled through the root-like joists and my every fibre thrilled with the hostility of those timber brakes.

The first of the boards I laid at right angles to the joist. I then drove two-inch nails through the heavy sheet, down into balk and beam, the joist and noggin that comprised the supporting structure. Restricted in the free movement of my limbs in those cramped conditions, the first strike of the hammer fell false, the nail bent and, discovering the instrument of their burial to be without claw, I was unable to extract the nail from the board whose vicelike grip now held it fast so I beat the nail down, flattening its deformity into the floor-grade chipboard until it could scarce be seen.

So I continued, staggering the boards like brickwork, single-minded in my desire to produce a work that would astound the doctor with its thoroughness. I glued each joint generously and, using a block of wood between the hammer and the sheet material, so as not to damage the tongue, I beat the next board close so that the glue oozed and bubbled from the sutures as blood from a wound. With a damp cloth I wiped away this excess before it could scab and dry.

Time and again the hammer swung, driven by my own loco-motion, tracing its relentless arc, striking at times on steel, at others on wood, sending the metal fixings vibrating deep into the board. In time I noted that five or six such vibrations or blows would bring the head of each nail level with the surface of the chipboard and by dint of my toil the boards increased their dominion over the wooden framework, to sink finally like fangs biting one by one to close and lock their prey in a deathly grip.

How many hours I crawled on my knees about that low timber framework I could not say. At times some breath or vapour threatened to extinguish the flickering light and in those moments I feared to step blindly into the void, to crash through the fragile plasterwork, that lay like a trap all about me, falling to I know not what fate and to what additional labours.

At others, hearing the echoes of my blows resound in that dark vault, I desisted from my labours, imagining a sound or presence there behind me in the shadows. Sometimes I remained perfectly still, listening in the gloom, nor saw I aught, but the malignant echo continued my companion, its metallic and clangorous reverberation, muffled as though at great distance, unerring as it beat a counterpoint that made itself felt in the hairs on the back of my neck.

The day wore on and with each passing hour the expanse of chipboard spread about me like the incoming tide. Soon I found I could walk freely in those areas new boarded. My hands and knees rejoiced in their newfound freedom, and I felt the blood return to my tired limbs. I lost all sense of time, but feeling the air grow cold I knew that night had fallen over the vacant fields of rank sedge that surrounded the lonely old house. I now thrilled to think of the space I had created in that antre, vast and idle, wherein my precious collection would take its place. I judged each board sufficient in length and breadth to hold a year's collection; soon there would be space enough to hold the records of a lifetime, the catalogue of death and folly that I kept as a warning to my fellow actuaries.

In time the smell of glue and treated wood, oppressive to my respiration, hung thick in the still air, but on I toiled, limbs aching, palms and fingers tender from long handling of the boards, their rough edges so unlike the smooth files and documents that comprised the responsibilities of my professional life. I proceeded here with the same diligence of action, with the same obsessive energy that so characterised my research – I resolved to leave not one square foot fallow in the large and lofty chamber. My tired eyes, however, fought now to reach the remoter angles of the chamber, the recesses where I struggled to fit the last pieces of the puzzle. As my labours drew to their diabolic conclusion I pulled the lantern close to the area in which I now fitted the final boards. Its sulphurous lustre cast long shadows on the angled surfaces about me and I saw the black shadow of the hammer held in my fist aloft, yet whether through inanition or some strange flickering of the flame the shadow appeared to begin its descent before its parent.

Making haste to keep pace, my own blow missed its mark and I recoiled in pain. As I clutched at the engorged extremity my involuntary motion caused the lantern to fall, spilling fuel and flame onto the fresh dry wood, made more flammable by the gaseous fumes of the adhesive. The flame caught; in moments I would have been engulfed, had I hesitated to smother the conflagration with my own hands and body. The smell of burnt hair and flesh filled my nostrils, but my swift reaction had extinguished the fire. I rolled back, my eyes trying in vain to pierce that ebon darkness, and cradling my injured hands I struggled towards the hatch that led to the comfort of my living quarters below. No feeble gleam relieved the profundity of that primeval gloom and my blistered fingers now began to feel their way across the new flooring, tracing each seam and joint towards the centre of that domelike cavern. The miasmatic vapours that rose from the drying glue lay like a mist on my blind path and the incubus of alarm settled on my soul. As I continued my course, my fingers probing ahead into the gloom like the antennae of some great insect, my sense of dread accelerated until a long low groan involuntarily escaped from my lungs. For you, reader, to conceive of the horror of my sensations is, I presume, utterly impossible. Time after time I extended my arm, hoping and praying to feel the void beneath me, the open hatch that would free me from this infernal chamber, so that now I would have rejoiced to find myself falling headlong to injury and freedom, even death. But at every turn my blind probing fell upon the resistance of well-fitted, floor-grade chipboard, made fast by my own labours.

Long days have passed since I laid the deck of the unbreachable hold in which I make my final voyage. Cargo-like I sprawl, my leg, most unnatural in its configuration, broken in the fall from the roofbeam. In the darkness I lie twice blinded; my senseless fingers, torn and bleeding from long hours spent scratching and tearing at joint and nail, my eyes redundant in the darkness. My strength, following that long departed cherub, Hope, is gone. My nerves have been unstrung.

I am woken from sleep, no! from swoon, from delirium. A single beam of light falls on my sunken countenance. Ha ha, through the slateless crevice, made before my fall, I see his eye peering down. I hear the flapping of his dark wings, the scratching of his clawlike toes. My parched lips, bitter from sucking at the damp and glue-soaked cloth, writhe in welcome with a senseless locution.

The hateful eye watches me now almost constantly. I see him. And I hear his kindred, gathering on the rooftop. An unkindness of ravens, waiting, waiting to gather me up, parcel by parcel. I can write no more. Dear Doctor, ensure this record finds its way into my collection. Then set a match to them all.

The Great Red Porcupine Trapped in the Snake Pit, Narco Guerrilla Gardening

OR

Putting Up a Garden Fence

with Hunter S. Thompson

TOOLS:

Spade or post auger
Spirit level
Hammer
Saw

MATERIALS:

Fence posts
Arris rails
Featheredge boards
Post mix or sand cement and hardcore
Nails
Brackets

Putting Up a Garden Fence

To my mind the corvette convertible is the only vehicle that can carry a ten-foot length of timber in style, but when it comes to making a handbrake turn or high-speed manoeuvres in excess of a hundred miles per hour, it begins to show its limitations as a serious hauler of lumber. By the time we arrived back at the house the car looked like it had been involved in a high-speed collision with Uncle Tom's Cabin. As I lowered the volume on Dylan's "Subterranean Homesick Blues" and extricated myself from the woodpile I could hear the voice of my attorney somewhere in the thicket of timbers that had sprouted in the seat next to me: "Man, this is no way to travel." What remained of the ten ten-foot arris rails, five ten-foot gravel boards, eighty four-foot featheredge boards and six eight-foot four-inch by four-inch sawn posts we'd stacked so neatly in the bucket seat was now piled against the windshield. In the trunk six bags of post mix (a lethal concoction of ready-mixed hardcore, sand and cement), twenty brackets and six pounds of nails made the car's nose point skyward so that it looked like a giant red porcupine was trying to climb up onto the sidewalk. It was important to keep my attorney's spirits up while I assessed his chances of survival. "Sweet Jesus, don't you just love the smell of fresh-cut timber in the morning?" I asked. "Can you move your legs?"

"Fuck no. I'm paralysed, call a doctor, a real doctor. Those bastards from the Pentagon have been testing some kind of napalm down at Bob's Premier Sheds and Fencing. My leg won't bend." Sure enough the Samoan's leg was rigid as I pulled it out across the passenger seat. Something was protruding from just above the knee and I feared that, in the emergency stop, he had suffered an open fracture. In his current state I doubted he was capable, but as a doctor I had to ask, "Are you in pain?"

"I can't feel a fucking thing."

"That's good." He needed to be reassured. "The bone has probably cut straight through the nerve." His screaming was cut short when he saw the neighbour peering from the window. "What's that old bitch looking at?" Now that he'd stopped screaming I felt emboldened to investigate the wound. "Hold still," I said, sliding the blade of an eight-inch hunting knife up his trouser leg and opening the fabric to the knee.

"How does it look?" he asked, still looking up at the house.

"You'll walk again." I put on my best $800 a day (TV not inclusive) bedside manner and removed the four-foot featheredge board that had somehow inserted itself in the great Samoan's trouser leg. "The pants, however, might not make it."

"This is my best fucking suit. Who's going to employ me like this? ARE YOU HAPPY NOW?" This last comment was screamed at the window of the clapboard villa where my neighbours were no doubt already calling the police.

When he'd recovered the feeling in his legs we unloaded the materials onto the lawn. I drove a wooden peg into the ground at each end of the fence run and stretched a line between. I then marked the position of the fence posts, avoiding tree roots and landmines. I instructed my attorney to start digging and waited for the mescaline to kick in.

As the Samoan slammed his spade into the ground he stopped to look back over his shoulder. "There's someone watching us," he said.

"It'll be the neighbour," I said. "It's a small town."

"As your attorney, I advise you to kill her. Once she's seen where we bury this stuff, what's to stop her coming over to dig it up after dark?"

The guy at the timber yard had told us if we buried one quarter of the post the rest should stand up well in a hurricane. "Don't worry," I said. "With six feet of post sticking out of the ground to mark where we buried the other two, I don't think this is a secret we can keep for long. Just keep digging, we don't want to look suspicious."

He lifted a size-eleven foot onto the spade, his leg peeking coquettishly through the slit trouser leg, and the blade sank into the ground. There was a lot to do. As project leader my immediate task was to recover the quart of Wild Turkey we had left on the back seat of the car.

At some point after removing the top from the bottle I must have passed out. When I came round I could hear the dry thud of spade on earth and the rattle of pebbles against steel. My attorney was still digging. I looked out into the garden but he was nowhere to be seen. Holy shit, I thought, the sound of digging has burnt itself onto the retina of my ear. I'm cursed to hear it for ever, like the rhythm section of . . . Then I saw a flurry of dust fly up from the ground and the sound stopped.

"Help. Somebody fucking get me out of here!"

Either the mescaline had worn off or my attorney had reached a tricky point of law. I staggered out into the garden; as I reached the site of the first post, the empty bottle fell from my hand. The hole was now about seven feet deep and the eminent Samoan, still in his business suit, was thrashing at the ground and dancing, like his feet were on fire. "Snakes, they're coming up through the ground. As soon as I cut the head off one, another one appears. Get me out of here!"

Somehow I pulled him from the hole and the two of us lay panting for breath on the ground. "Don't worry," I said, "if it's long enough, we can beat them to death with the fence post."

To reassure the great excavator that the snakes would not be climbing out of the hole, and to add some much needed drainage, I threw the contents of a bucket of hardcore, mostly broken bricks and small stones, down into the depths, shouting, "Eat hardcore, you scaly motherfuckers."

By the time I looked up the Samoan was standing over me, stripped to the waist holding a shotgun. I had a perfect view of the inside of both barrels. "You filthy bastard," he said. "How long have you known about those snakes? I oughta blow your fucking head off." I was on my knees over a vertical grave deep enough to bury a man upright, two men even, if packed carefully, with a drug-crazed attorney in slit pants aiming a shotgun at my head. There were signs that I might be losing control of the situation.

"You're fired," I said.

"What do you mean, I'm fired?"

"As a qualified doctor I can see that you've not been taking your medication. I can't afford to carry sick men on this job."

"Oh, Jesus," he groaned, relaxing the gun into the crook of his arm, "I forgot." From his pocket the Samoan produced a salt cellar of cocaine and poured a line onto the back of his hand. When he'd finished walking his nose along the line he licked off the residue, sucked his teeth and said, "As your attorney, I advise you to mark the position of the next hole and stand aside."

Putting Up a Garden Fence

The spade was lying in the bottom of the snake pit but the Samoan knew that the refusal to give up is at the heart of the American Dream. He set his feet wide apart over the mark and, at close range, fired the shotgun straight down into the ground. There was no doubting his reasoning, a hole seemed the logical consequence. While I set out the blue floral sunloungers and mixed two more tequilas, he let off the second barrel and reloaded. Lying there I gazed dreamily up at the sunlight twinkling through the leaves. My eyelids hung heavy behind gold-rimmed shades as I sipped on my sunrise, listening to the explosive bass line of the Samoan's dirt shoot. Somewhere between cartridge twenty and fifty the tequila began to cut through the drugs. Fine luck it would be if the police now arrived at the door.

"You say you're a doctor? Well, now, doctor, you more than anyone should be aware that a twelve-bore shotgun is not a suitable tool to be used when erecting a fence."

"I'm sorry, officer, but this was an urgent case. The neighbour's dog has been pissing on my marijuana, I mean my dahlia collection. We worked its owner over so badly with the spade that now it doesn't dig straight. Perhaps you could lend a hand."

What happened next convinced me that somehow, in between the wood yard and the house, probably when we swerved at high speed to avoid the crazy guy in the wheelchair on the sidewalk, we had entered, like Connecticut Yankees, some weird kind of Twain's World.

Someone was ringing the doorbell, they were desperate to see us and weren't going away. Through the side light in the hall I could see a patrol car parked behind the porcupine. "It's the cops," I said.

The Samoan offered me the shotgun. "As your attorney, I advise you not to be taken alive." He was still twisted, but I persuaded him to drop the weapon into the snake hole and remove the salt cellar from his left nostril.

When faced with a house call from the police never greet them politely – this will only arouse suspicion in the cop gut. The thing to do is to launch immediately into the role of the indignant citizen and demand an explanation. "What the hell kept you, officer? I could have been killed, he must have fired off sixty rounds before we chased him into the shrubbery. He could still be hiding in the potting shed."

I opened the door to face my accusers; two patrolmen were brandishing a stack of four-foot featheredge board. Holy shit, Bob's Premier Sheds and Fencing is supplying the police department too. My brain locked up, but my mouth was already loose. "He's still in the garden, officer, I think he'll come quietly now." It looked like I'd have to get my hands dirty on this one and my chief excavator was about to be buried.

The cop laughed. "Seriously, sir, a load should be properly fastened before you go on the highway. We followed the trail of timber to the wood store where they gave us your address and a description of your vehicle. A convertible is not suitable for the transportation of large loads of timber. Would you mind letting us in, this stuff's getting heavy."

I thought I was hallucinating. For the first time in my life I'd found a cop who was trying to protect and serve, home delivery included. The great magnet was pulling in my direction and it felt good.

"So what brings you guys to the neighbourhood? You're

new around here, right?" They dropped the boards onto the lawn and then saw my attorney. He was crouched over the pit, his head moving from side to side in a snakelike motion.

"Wow, that's a hell of a foundation you've dug there."

The Samoan was back on his feet. "Doctor, let me take care of this. Tell room service we'll need coffee." He took the patrolmen by the arm and began speaking in a whisper. "The good doctor here is a key part in the war on drugs and terror. In order to help combat the nationwide threat to the American way of life, he needs total quiet."

"No shit. You hear that, Ed? The doc's a big shot. Why is he here? We don't really have much of a problem with that stuff in Oatville."

"Oh, it's coming." I handed round coffee and offered the patrolmen some doughnuts that I'd found in the kitchen. The Samoan took a handful and began filling his pockets. "He hasn't had breakfast," I said apologetically.

The Samoan then snatched the last doughnut from my hand and continued his exposé: "Don't you guys read the papers? A hard rain's gonna fall and it's heading this way. If the doctor here doesn't succeed, your kids could all be dope fiends within a year. Why do you think we're fixing this fence? Here, hold this." While one of the cops held the post in a hole full of shot, my attorney used the spirit level to check it was straight. "Your people need to wake up or gangs of twisted junkies are going to be moving in all over the county. Officers, can I trust you?" Their mouths still full with doughnut, the two men nodded. The Samoan gave instructions to Officer Squane to pour one of the bags of cement mix in around the base of the four-inch by four-inch post and add a bucket of water. I mixed another round of tequilas and cleared the cups. I had yet to lay my hands on anything heavier than a cocktail stick and intended to keep it that way. I have no objection to heavy work, but I couldn't interfere with the workings of the great magnet.

The team kept working until all the posts were in the ground. As the cement was drying my attorney filled in the details of the plot against America.

"The producers can't grow their evil harvest on open farmland, that would be playing into the hands of the feds, and the crop-dusting air service, so they're growing the stuff in the homes of innocent Americans. Oh, yeah, Miss Maudie doesn't recognise that plant growing in her azaleas? You're sure as hell right she don't! She's part of the problem. That grade A narcotic harvest is growing in the gardens of America."

"Can you believe this stuff, Ed? What the hell's happening to this country?" I watched them listening to the Samoan's impassioned plea.

"It's not just the neighbour's dog walking through the hole in that fence. We're talking about a gateway to oblivion, a portal through which a million short-circuited, fucked-up, smack-headed freak kings are gonna be walking out onto the streets of this proud land. The stuff's not being smuggled over the border; it's not coming up the Hudson in a submarine; they're picking it straight from Miss Maudie's azalea patch. And no one's even watching. While we're watching the borders, these guerrilla narco gardeners are taking over the ground under our feet."

Patrolman Ed was strangely afflicted and starting to get

jumpy. He had already begun cutting the rails to fit between the posts and it wasn't long before his okie partner was using the brackets to help the Samoan nail them into place.

"Hot damn, Ed! We better warn Old Man Mitchell. His fence is still down from that storm last September."

The police did everything they could to assist my attorney. The rails were now all in place and as the gravel boards were nailed to wooden cleats at the bottom of each post, the sound of hammering followed me into the kitchen. My legal team then began hammering the boards to the rails, until a call on the radio meant that we were left to finish off the last few without the protection of our local boys in blue. The hard work seemed to have taken its toll, they both looked kind of rubbery as they headed for their patrol car. The younger of the two, Ed, fell over as he tried to draw his handgun when a large shrub on the front lawn blocked his path. "Officer," I said to his partner, "this is all still highly confidential, we can't have the press getting hold of this story. I'd appreciate it if you didn't talk about this meeting." Their car lurched into reverse before driving off, weaving from side to side. I was laughing crazily as I stepped back into the house. "I think we should put them on the payroll," I said to my attorney.

"They could be looking for a job by the morning."

"What do you mean?"

"Those doughnuts you handed out."

"Yeah, what about them?"

"I wasn't expecting visitors, they were meant to be for us." I began to fear the worst. "I injected them with mescaline."

"You did what? A mescaline jam mix, that's a lethal

concoction. I wouldn't want to be in Old Man Mitchell's shoes once that stuff kicks in. What are we going to do?"

"As your attorney I advise you to take this." From his pocket he then handed me a doughnut. I felt the jam running down my chin and a wave of happiness engulfed me as the mournful wail of a police siren drifted in over the fence on the evening breeze.

Applying Sealant Round a Bath

with Johann Wolfgang von Goethe

TOOLS:
Mastic gun
Small wedge-shaped piece of wood

MATERIALS:
Silicone sealant
Washing-up liquid

22 May

Oh, my dear friend. What a thing our human destiny is! How happy I am to be embarking on a life in the country at last! Though I cannot say that I have yet met with any society, the solitude here is a balm, and I have already made all manner of acquaintance. A local handyman has become attached to me and will not have cause to regret it. Yesterday I sketched him replacing the guttering on a neighbour's house. I liked his way so spoke to him and asked after his circumstances. Presently we were acquainted and soon, as generally happens to me with this kind of person, intimate. What a serenity has taken possession of my soul since I arrived here in these paradisic parts.

Today he paid me a visit and was kind enough to suggest a large number of improvements to the property, all of which, he assures me, he is more than able to assist with.

25 May

Thank you, my friend, for your warning. Though I well know he can never be my equal, my workman appears an honest type with most pleasing features and attitude. I shall scarcely be able to tell you with what enthusiasm he began work on the house. He is an open man of good heart and I see no reason to keep my distance for the sake of form.

On his suggestion I have paid him in advance and provided him with a set of keys. While I was away riding he removed that old iron bathtub, preparatory to replacing it with a magnificent modern bath and shower unit of such harmonious shape and proportion that my very soul is afire, longing and languishing to try it.

On my return, soaked and dirty from one of those early summer showers that strike with so little notice, the water supply was cut off, but the worthy fellow showed such grace and generosity in sharing with me the contents of his flask of coffee that I was reminded of that magnificent passage in Homer where Odysseus enjoys the hospitality of the excellent swineherd. What fools men are not to see the obstacles that class and privilege place before us.

29 May

How these beautiful spring mornings fill the heart. Today finally the young fellow returned. I cannot express the feelings that overwhelmed me as he busied himself installing the bathtub I described to you in my last letter. Indeed, I should need the gifts of the greatest poets if I were to recount his expressive gestures, the harmony and economy of his movement and the secret fire that shone in his eyes as he set about laying the copper pipes, shaping them to fit so neatly the contours of the room and using his blow torch to such brilliant effect.

The sight delighted me and I sat down on the toilet seat across from him and took great pleasure in drawing this domestic idyll. I added the tiles that formed a backdrop to his work, a towel and the sink, all simply the way it was. And I must congratulate myself on creating a harmonious study. Surely there is more of dignity and honour in one hour of manual labour than in a month of observing protocol and ceremony in the service of the ambassador.

6 June

I no longer know where I got to in my story. It has been more than a week now since I last saw my artisan. A few of his tools still lie abandoned on the bathroom floor, some small wooden wedges, a simple mastic gun and a tube of white silicone sealant. A jar, containing a solution of washing-up liquid, sits still on the window ledge. How their presence haunts me.

I supposed at first that he had perhaps taken ill, until today, when I caught sight of his van in front of another house in the vicinity. I waited for some time to speak with him. When finally, giving up hope, I left a note and walked on, a shout of laughter could be heard from the window. I could tear my heart open and beat my poor head on seeing how little people can mean to each other.

I grind my teeth; the devil take him! Ah, I have snatched up the gun a hundred times thinking to relieve my sorely beset heart.

11 June

Ah this void, this terrible void I feel in my breast. Still no reply or sign of progress. God knows how often I have regretted ever beginning this course of action. Woe! As ever, I fear you are right my friend. Toil and labour, joys and rewards, they cannot be separated.

14 June

The decision is taken. A thousand possibilities and plans raged in my heart but in the end it was there, one last fixed and definite thought. The gun is now in my hand and I am resolved to do whatever is necessary.

Applying Sealant Round a Bath

I placed the tube of sealant snugly in the mastic gun and, using only a simple pair of scissors, removed the extremity from the tube's tapered nozzle, so that, when squeezed, the amalgam, as white as the driven snow, was greater in girth than the gap between bath and tiles. What I told you recently concerning painting I can confirm is also true of applying bath sealant; what counts is that one conceives of a line of perfect breadth and straightness, and then dares to give it expression. Applying the steadiest of pressure to the trigger, I began, at one end of the bath, to lay down a steady flow of the sealant, and so to fill the abyss that had tortured me for so long. Then, from among the little wooden wedges I chose one, the width of my little fingernail, and put it to soak in the jar containing the washing-up solution before drawing it with a smooth and steady motion along the little ribbon of white that now joined bath and wall as one. I swear that every man should pass a few moments of each day in such common labour. Its simple pleasure is a balm to the heart.

Farewell. This letter will be to your taste, it is full of practical steps.

That evening I lay soaking in my tub. Through the window, above the chestnut trees illuminated in the moonlight, shone the stars that make up the blade of the Plough, my favourite and the most practical of all the heavenly bodies. But of all this I was hardly sensible. What overwhelmed me with emotion and made the world about me a very paradise, was the blue-white gleam of the sealant in the moonlight, its edges so straight, its surface a smooth and perfect barrier betwixt tile and tub, holding back the splashing foam that burst from the banks of the bath. In such moments the humblest labourer, fatigued by his exertions, surely floats more buoyantly on the waters of the measureless sea, soaks more deeply in the foaming pool of the Eternal and approaches more closely the blessed serenity of Him who makes all things.

Remedying a Drawer that Sticks

with Samuel Beckett

MATERIALS:
Wax candle

ACT ONE

Two figures on a country road. Grey light fading to darkness. Between them, atop a small mound, sits a chest of drawers. The figure on the left, CONNOR, wears dark glasses; he is blind and carries a stick. On the right, GODARD. Both are looking at the piece of furniture.

GODARD. What are you waiting for? You won't find better. It's a lovely piece of work.

CONNOR. (*Stroking his hand along the surface of the chest and cocking his ear forward to listen.*) Yes. Yes it is.

GODARD. It was made by my father you know.

CONNOR. Really. I never knew. (*Running his hands over the front of the cabinet.*) It could be just what I need.

GODARD. Believe me, a lovely piece of work.

CONNOR. Did it take him long?

GODARD. About a week I think, he made a lot of things.

CONNOR. It could do the job nicely. (*Feeling his way, he starts to walk round to the other side of the chest. As he walks GODARD places his hands on the chest and turns it, moving round so that though the two men exchange places, the front is always facing CONNOR. The back of the chest is covered with hardboard and has a hole. CONNOR looks up momentarily from the chest towards GODARD.*) How much did you say you were looking for?

GODARD. You can't put a value on something like this, it has sentimental connotations. A man's work you know. I want it to go to a good home, somewhere that it will be cherished.

CONNOR. Yes, yes, of course. A man's work. Would you mind? ... (*CONNOR gestures with his hand to the front of the drawer.*)

GODARD. Not at all. Not at all, please. (*He steps forward, reaching for CONNOR's arm to help.*)

CONNOR. (*Pushing him off angrily.*) Don't you touch me. I can do it.

(*There is no handle on the drawer. For a while CONNOR searches for the handle, then tries to grip the drawer by its edges. Bent low, his head resting against the chest of drawers, he listens, his fingers moving slowly around the joints in the wood. Finally his face looks up in appeal. For a moment GODARD looks at him blankly, then looks more closely at CONNOR's dark glasses, then starts into action. He searches through his pockets, pulls forth a screwed-up handkerchief and unwraps it to reveal a brass knob, which he then screws to a thread that protrudes at the front on the drawer. Delicately he places CONNOR's hands on the handle.)*

GODARD. There you go.

CONNOR. That's more like it. (*He rubs his hands together, then pulls on the handle without success. Surprised.*) What have you got in here? (*Breathing heavily, he tries again, this time spitting on his hands before rubbing them together. He rattles the handle and tries once more.*) It won't budge.

GODARD. (*Irritated.*) You're not pulling it straight. Get out the way. (*He pushes CONNOR to one side, then pulls on the handle, increasing his effort but without success.*) Well, lend a hand.

(*CONNOR holds GODARD round the waist and the two men pull. After much heaving and shouting the drawer opens about two inches.*)

GODARD. There. What did I say? You just have to pull it straight.

CONNOR. (*Feeling the opening with his fingers.*) It's not exactly open, is it.

GODARD. It's not *exactly* closed.

CONNOR. You say your father made this?

GODARD. How dare you.

CONNOR. (*Attempting to move the drawer.*) Don't you think it's a bit stiff?

GODARD. It just needs a bit of wax. (*GODARD peers into the open drawer, then reaches his fingers into the opening. He leans the chest forward; a sound of rolling comes from the drawer. CONNOR looks up at the sky.*)

CONNOR. Sounds like rain.

GODARD. Got it. (*In order to use both hands he releases the chest, which falls back upright. Again the sound of rolling, again CONNOR looks skywards, worried. GODARD looks at him with contempt.*) Are you just going to stand there? Push the chest this way. (*Slowly CONNOR stops looking up and goes to the back of the chest of drawers to lean it towards GODARD. Again the sound of rolling. CONNOR looks mournfully upwards at the sky.*)

CONNOR. Is it getting dark?

GODARD. What's the date?

CONNOR. June the twenty-second.

GODARD. The nights are drawing in.

CONNOR. Is it night yet?

GODARD. (*Still peering in at the opening.*) I couldn't say. There, I've got it. (*He pulls from the drawer a large white candle.*) That'll do the trick. (*Bent low, he begins to rub the candle against the sides of the drawer and closes it with his shoulder.*) Voilà.

CONNOR. Have you shut it again?

GODARD. I have.

CONNOR. After all that?

GODARD. Try it. (*He gestures towards the drawer, then places CONNOR's hands on the handle. Unconvinced, CONNOR grasps the handle with both hands and braces himself for a great effort. The drawer comes free with ease and CONNOR falls back, holding the drawer.*) See the quality of the work-manship. Those drawers were made to last.

(*Still lying on the floor, CONNOR examines the joints on the drawer with admiration.*)

CONNOR. Dovetails, that's quality. (*He taps the drawer.*

Places it on its end on the ground, then raises himself and sits down on it.) So what are we talking about here?

GODARD. Let me wax the runners. (*He reaches into the space left by the drawer and rubs the candle along the two runners that sit either side of the drawer.*) She'll handle like a dream now. (*He steps back and gestures again to the opening.*) Try putting it back now.

CONNOR. (*Returns the drawer to the space and cautiously closes it.*) May I? (*A smug nod from GODARD. Delicately CONNOR opens the drawer then begins to fill it with the contents of his right-hand pocket, an enormous quantity of underpants, until the drawer is full to overflowing. He then leans his shoulder against it and closes the drawer with effort.*) Like a dream.

(*GODARD stands the candle in the middle of the chest of drawers and lights it with a match.*)

Curtain

ACT TWO

Scene as before. Light lower. The chest of drawers and the mound lit, fading to darkness elsewhere on the stage. The candle is still burning. CONNOR is kneeling before the chest of drawers, his hands moving over the drawer fronts as though searching for something.

CONNOR. I said I don't need your help. I can do this on my own. (*GODARD remains standing silent. He takes off his hat and looks inside it. Puts it back on his head and adjusts it.*

CONNOR's movements become more frustrated.) Well, lend a hand. Lend a hand! Can't you see I need help? She's stuck fast.

GODARD. Try one of the other drawers.

CONNOR. I don't want to look in one of the other drawers. I want to look in the bottom drawer.

GODARD. It hasn't been opened in a long time.

CONNOR. What use is a drawer that can't be opened?

GODARD. For tidying things out the way. Like a memory you can't remember.

CONNOR. A memory you can't remember? Do you mean like time lost?

GODARD. Like dirt flushed down the pan.

CONNOR. What if somebody else remembers it?

GODARD. Not the same. Two people can't have the same memory.

CONNOR: (*Struggling still with the drawer front*.) Well, a drawer that can't be opened isn't a drawer.

GODARD. It did once. It was a source of great joy.

CONNOR. (*Pulling hard*.) This?

GODARD. Oh, how often she would sit looking into that bottom drawer. (*Pause*.) Fine linens, lacework, napkins. All embroidered by her own fair hand. Did you ever see such delicate fingers? What hopes were harboured in that little chest. The fine dinners that she planned, white tulips opening in spring sunlight as it falls across the lace-draped oak chiffonier. The hand-knitted jacket and booties lovingly fastened with a ribbon. What dreams dwelt in its lined and scented walls.

CONNOR. You've remembered.

GODARD. Who needs memories.

CONNOR. Happy memories.

GODARD. Most painful of all.

CONNOR. (*Still struggling with the drawer.*) You'll have to help me.

(*GODARD falls to his knees beside CONNOR. They take turns alternately screwing the handle on at each side of the wide drawer. The handle is passed back and forth between them, opening the drawer an inch at a time, until the drawer is open.*)

CONNOR. Gogo. There's something in it. It might be something to eat.

GODARD. I don't think so. Let's close it. Before night falls.

CONNOR. (*Looking skywards.*) Night is falling?

GODARD. Falling quickly.

CONNOR. (*Leaning forward and reaching into the drawer*) Fine woollens. Delicate filigree of embroidery on fine cotton. (*Hopefully.*) There's a little bone, wrapped in muslin. A leg. (*Disappointed.*) There's not much meat on it. (*GODARD removes his hat and holds it with both hands against his breast.*) Material crumbling to dust. (*Slowly.*) Silken strands of hair. (*Pause. CONNOR removes his hat too and holds it over his chest.*)

Curtain

ACT THREE

Scene as before. Though darker, the chest of drawers is now partly buried so that the bottom drawer is no longer visible. CONNOR, crawling on all fours, pats the earth down. GODARD, standing, holds a shovel and uses it to do the same. The candle still burns.

CONNOR. Words fail me.

GODARD. There was nowhere else to put him.

CONNOR. Has night fallen yet?

GODARD. (*Looking up.*) Nearly.

CONNOR. Are there stars?

GODARD. No.

CONNOR. Not one can be seen?

GODARD. (*He looks again.*) No.

CONNOR. But they're there?

GODARD. If you say so.

CONNOR. I can smell them burning.

GODARD. It's the candle.

CONNOR. (*Looking up with hope.*) Twinkling above?

GODARD. Sort of.

> (*CONNOR attaches the handle to the lowest of the drawers still visible. He pulls the drawer out from the chest, produces another candle from his pocket and waxes each side of the drawer, turning it upside down before pushing it partially back into the chest and sliding it back and forth testing its movement. He repeats the process with each of the remaining drawers, closing them each slightly further to create a set of steps.*)

CONNOR. Will you help me up. (*He offers his arm to GODARD.*) I was going to say a prayer.

GODARD. (*Cheerily*) A prayer? Good God.

CONNOR. Tell me. I've been meaning to ask you. What keeps you from hanging yourself?

GODARD. She used to ask me that. After he ... Before she ...

Before ... (*Pause.*) I've always been a late developer. (*He rises from his knees, takes CONNOR's arm and begins to climb the steps.*)

CONNOR. Watch the varnish! It'll come up nicely with a bit of beeswax. (*GODARD reaches the top of the chest, removes his hat and holds it across his chest in a statuesque pose. CONNOR meanwhile empties the contents of his left pocket, a pile of socks, onto the ground and begins tying them end to end.*)

GODARD. (*Abandoning his pose.*) What are you doing?

CONNOR. (*Not pausing in his activity.*) I'm making you a rope.

GODARD. With your stinking socks?

CONNOR. It won't be for long, I'll hang on to your legs.

GODARD. You'd do that for me?

CONNOR. You'd have done as much for me.

GODARD. That I would, Coco. Go on then, I'll have it as a scarf, it'll be cold up here.

CONNOR. Then you're not going to jump?

GODARD. I'll just keep watch (*Resuming the statuesque pose.*) and wait.

Curtain

Unblocking a Sink

with Jean-Paul Sartre

TOOLS:
Plunger
Bucket
Wire
Cloth

MATERIALS:
None

Monday 0700

Something has happened. So cunningly did it instil itself that at first I doubted my own senses. Even just now bent over the white hollowed form, I became aware of a slight feeling of awkwardness. The black and grey specks of hair shaved from my face float on the surface of the water, mixing at its edges with the residue of cheap soap to form a kind of scum or crust that attaches itself slowly to the basin as though drawn by some kind of residual magnetism.

Unblocking a Sink

The water level in the sink now descends so slowly it can scarcely be perceived by the eye, its movement can only be measured by the progress of the grey residue that coats itself onto the smooth white porcelain. Like the deposit of words and letters spawned by my pen, gathering without significance on the chalk-white paper.

Like a throat in paralysis, the sink will not swallow, it will not take any more of the filth that it has been forced to drink for so long. I look into the dark vent, straining my eyes to see what has fouled the pipe. Something glistens in the dark; the filmy surface of an eye, round and wet, is looking back at me. A foul smell emanates from the throat, an odour of sickness, nausea. I won't stand for it. I won't. The glistening surface disappears and the eye closes. There, in the filth it has come, the Blockage.

Outside in the rue des Martyrs the shopkeepers are opening their doors, a group of men ending the night shift file into the brothel, their voices gargling and bubbling as they disappear one by one into the darkness of the interior. A woman emerges from the church. Dressed in black, she turns three times in a spiral before disappearing into the shadows of the narrow street that runs alongside the west wing of the church.

I leave the apartment to take my place in the ebb and flow. A bell rings and I hear the sound of shoes on bare floorboards, the smell of paraffin, paint, varnish. On the counter a small fleshy white creature lies on its back, its feet in the air in an attitude of submission. A second creature approaches, grasping an object in its paws. It appears to mount the first and as they brush against each other deposits something on its belly. The first rights itself and withdraws. A second bell chimes, the till is closed. I have paid. Brown paper rustles as it enfolds the awkwardly shaped object I have bought. The ironmonger, the same man who cut the key I had made for Anny before she left, hands me the irregular-shaped package. I see that the second of the creatures still hangs suspended in the air, it is my hand, it retreats to the dark warmth of my pocket where I feel its weight against my thigh.

Thursday morning in the Library

Things are bad, very bad. I cannot work. Every movement of my pen is without significance. My novel bores me. I have not energy even to fill my pipe. The object sits in front of me, where it draws the attention of the librarian. The Blockage has taken hold of me.

1630

Now unwrapped, the object sits on the counter next to the sink. A black hemisphere made of rubber, attached to a wooden handle. As though to reassure myself that it has not all been a dream, I run the tap and wait. There is no happy gurgling, no rush of water speeding down a pipe, to fall, unseen, as it passes through the apartments of the neighbours below. No, the water collects in the sink. I place the rubber dome over the plughole, block the overflow with a damp cloth and, using both hands, press down on the handle. The rubber hemisphere gives way and becomes a hemitoroid. It holds fast and I pull the stick back and forth, my arms jerking and flexing as the handle of the plunger moves like a piston in a cylinder.

My hands are shaking and the blood has rushed to my head. The plunger stands erect, dark water trailing over the bulbous rubber onto the counter. The plug still hangs by its chain from the tap, but the water level does not fall. The plunger does not work.

Beneath the sink there is a cupboard. Behind the mothballs and light bulbs, in the darkness beyond the scourers, cloths and washing powder, a white pipe forms the letter U. The letter brings to mind all that remains undone or has been reversed: Undone, Unloved, Unbroken, Undigested, Unforgotten, Unforgiven. Its two extremities are each attached by a threaded collar to a continuous pipe. My hands fumble in the dark space, loosening one of the collars. Already dirty water begins to seep from the broken seal. It trickles down the pipe to splash onto the packets of mothballs. As I come closer to the source of the Blockage my nostrils overflow with the putrid smell. The Blockage is everywhere.

I remove everything from the cupboard and place a bucket beneath the U-bend. I can now taste the Blockage. Like something dead and unburied it is in my mouth, my ears, my eyes. My stomach heaves. Fat white fingers move like grubs, rising and falling as they unfasten the collar. The little grooves of the thread show themselves one by one as the collar turns, like a needle on the surface of a record, bringing to life the voice of a long-dead singer. The U-bend comes away; water, putrid and grey, splashes onto my sleeve. I hold the U-shaped piece of plastic upside down; it is now an N-shape. The foul water pours into the bucket but nothing else emerges. The Blockage is still there, hiding in the bend. I am afraid to look. I do not want to see what has been growing in there, like a boil on the flesh until it is ready to burst. I am afraid. I am afraid of seeing again that viscous eye looking back at me. But I know I will look.

Slowly my hands bring the pipe towards me. The smell is overwhelming. Its extremities, now like two huge nostrils, blocked by a black horrible mass; vegetation that has crept up the drains from beyond the city limits, stretching its tentacles, its pincers, reaching closer into the life of the city that it seeks to reclaim. I push a piece of wire into one of the nostrils, pressing against the resistance of the Blockage, until it is forced from its nest and lands with a slap in the sink. Water oozes from the dark knot, I hear it drip into the bucket below. I reconnect the U-bend, tightening it by hand, and run the tap. The water lands in the sink, coating the surface, tracing a tangent, a curve, a spiral. The water thunders and the sink drinks and sings like a sailor, its thirst now unquenchable. The flow forms a continuum; if I run the tap long enough it will create an unbroken link between the reservoir and the sewage works, perhaps even a continuous loop, discontinuous only in respect of its filth. My intersection in this loop marks the point where the water becomes polluted, like my intervention in the life of Anny.

Under the force of the water the dark mass begins to break up, each of its components escapes a little at a time. Pieces of cabbage, fish scales, tea leaves wash away, leaving an animal-like nucleus of black hair swirling in the water. It is not mine,

Unblocking a Sink

my hair is short and red turning to grey; it is Anny's. I take up the disgusting clump and hold it in my hands. It feels alive. I pick at the last of the fish scales still caught in its mesh. I catch sight of myself in the mirror, grooming the strands like a monkey. What am I doing?

1830

Night has fallen. Below in the street the lights are now on in the Café Mably. I throw the clump of hair into the waste bin, unfasten the chain to open the door and begin to descend the winding staircase. The sound of my steps echoes in the narrow stairwell. At the second landing the lights go out. I stand still, unable to advance, my eyes blinking in the darkness. The small white light of a spyhole shines out in the door before me and then grows dark. Someone is watching, waiting for me to move, but I cannot. I am the Blockage.

Painting a Panelled Door

with Anaïs Nin

TOOLS:
Screwdriver
Brush

MATERIALS:
Primer
Undercoat
Gloss paint

She watched as he prised the lid from the paint, revealing the moonlike circle of white, into which he thrust the stiff animal bristle of his brush. His work was so sensual that women were attracted to him immediately. She had begun to court him, making little advances – talking about a lover in the past, or about the admiring glances she had received from the shopkeepers in the town. She lay back on the couch to watch him paint, her breasts thrust forward, her arms raised over her head. But the painter remained impassive; his passion found expression only in his work. Deep down she dreamed of a man who would rule her, take the lead sexually, yet the impassivity of the artist stirred her. Her admiration turned to love and she longed for him to make demands of her. When she looked at his strong hands and saw the paint beneath the nails, she yearned to feel their strength, to smell the perfume of turpentine and linseed rubbed onto her body, as he held her.

By night, as if in a dream, she walked the long corridors of the old hacienda, her body throbbing, as she sought the scent of fresh paint, eager to touch her fingers on its tacky surface. She was forced to become adventurous and bold. Each time she passed him at his work she brushed more closely by him, rejoicing to see the little flecks of paint smeared onto the smooth silk of her kimono. Finally she lost all reserve. Passing the painter in a doorway, she allowed her hand to brush against his brush. Suddenly he pushed her away, as if her gesture had insulted him. He looked proud, untouchable.

"What have I done?" she said.

"All this week you have watched me paint." His frown became a smile. "Now I will watch you." He handed her a brush, and pointed to the door, already stripped of its handle and brutally rubbed down earlier that day. "Paint."

Dressed in only her kimono, she now stood before the door, thrilling to feel the dark rectangle of stiff hair beneath her fingers.

"I said paint."

Observing her as she stood before him, he saw that she did not know how. Gently but firmly he directed her. Allowing her hand to be guided in his, she saw how the sticky white paint clung to the dark hair as she dipped the little brush into the open pot and ran the bristles along the edges of each panel. "First you must paint the mouldings in all the panels." As she followed his instructions the wet bristles began licking paint into every crevice and ornamentation, flicking against each curve until the paint grew thin and viscous.

Behind her she could hear the breathing of the painter. He observed the contractions of her muscles as she reached high, squeezing the brush tightly. "More paint," he commanded, watching now how her hips pushed towards him, her head held low, as she recharged her brush from the little pot of paint.

"Don't stop," he said. At the sound of his voice she pressed her brush to the door and a spurt of white paint trickled onto the floor. "You are pressing too hard. Be gentle, the gentlest of pressure and the brush will respond. Too much and the brush will spill its load. Clean it up now, with the cloth and the white spirit."

Feeling her body vibrate with unsatisfied desire, she obeyed his every command. The odours of turpentine, paint, of pinewood filled her senses and through their smell, so strong and penetrating, she felt his presence.

"Now paint the panels. Do not dip your brush too deeply into the paint."

She began to understand the rhythm he required of her, her body swaying with the movement of her arm. She could no longer see the painter but she sensed his eyes on her back, tracing the contours of her body beneath the silk of the kimono. She felt every stroke of the brush as though its pure bristle

197

were moving on the surface of her skin. Each movement in the paint created tiny currents and eddies, that she felt in her blood, watching as they disappeared in the paint, so wet, so inviting that she longed to touch it.

"When you have painted each panel stroke your brush along the grain." His breath came more heavily now and his voice fell lower in pitch. "Now to tackle the muntins." She imagined it to be a pet word of his, used for her breasts or thighs, and anticipated his strong hands taking her, but his long fingers pointed instead to the vertical pieces of wood at the centre of the door.

Now their breath kept time, little beads of sweat formed on her forehead and the painter's instruction grew more forceful; he seemed driven into a frenzy. "Next, the cross rails." He directed her hand to the three horizontal pieces of wood that helped to form the frame. "Here, *here* and HERE." His hair flew wildly as he swung his arms like the conductor of an orchestra. He seemed tireless and her arm ached with effort. What stamina he possessed, but she urged herself on, desiring only to give pleasure to her teacher, to give a good finish.

"Lay your brush against the stiles, the outer verticals that form the frame. You must work quickly, while it is still wet. Once it dries the bristles stick; it will leave the marks of the brush. Faster, faster."

With the last stroke she fell back, spent, her kimono lay open as her exhausted arm fell aslant her body, leaving a trickle of white paint across her flank.

The brush, she knew, would never tire, not until it had soaked up the last drop of paint. She lay trembling, her body naked, as the painter stood over her and uttered what she thought could not be possible. "Now is not the time to rest — you must clean your brush before it dries. For the second coat you will do it all again only with a better finish."

Great Writers in
the Garden

Introduction

with Niccolò Machiavelli

To the magnificent reader

Those who strive to obtain the good graces of a reader are accustomed to come before him with things in which they see him take most delight, whence one often reads adventures and romances, histories of great men and women, the struggles of the oppressed, or of the many ways in which a reader may improve his well-being or success.

Desiring no alteration in your magnificent person nor to distract you with stories I consider unworthy of your countenance, I now present you with this small volume containing that which I hold most dear: knowledge of the habits and actions of great gardeners and plantsmen and women. I offer to you in this short form all that I have learnt over long years of study with so many troubles and so much expense.

Nor have I embellished this work with the allurements and adornments with which so many are accustomed to embellish works of horticulture. If in the imparting of this knowledge I have drawn as much on my studies of the great writers as on my long experience as a gardener I make no apology. The reputation of a gardener, like that of a writer, is made on his ability to uproot the unwanted and cut down the superfluous.

Take, then, your Magnificence, this little gift. And if you take even some small pleasure from these tales of the parterre and the potager, you will see how I have with great and prolonged diligence sought only to win your favour and approval.

Planting a Hanging Basket

with Raymond Carver

TOOLS:
Hanging basket
Coir matting or liner
Compost
Slow release fertilizer
Plants
Water

That Saturday afternoon I was sitting on the sofa, reading the classifieds. You can learn a lot from reading the classifieds. Don't ask me what.

I was thinking about my mother. She'd written to say her TV was broke and she'd asked me to send her a little extra money that month. I'd agreed with Iris that I would call her that morning to tell her it was going to be difficult. "We've got troubles of our own," Iris said. "Why should we have to stake everyone?" she said. "What about your brother?" she said. "When did he last send any money?"

My brother hasn't got any money. She knows that. He stayed with us for a month back in the summer. He slept on the couch. He and Iris don't get along. Where he's staying now I don't even know.

"Your mother knows the plant closed," Iris says. "You told her, didn't you?"

"Sure I told her," I say. But my mother's old. She forgets. I waited until Iris was tidying in the kitchen before I made the call. Like she told me, I reminded my mother that I'd been terminated, that things were bad, but it didn't make any difference. My mother cried and said I was right to leave her to fend for herself. While she was talking I kept looking out the window, at the dead flowers in the hanging basket. In the end I said I'd send the money. Iris was listening as I made the call. She was still tidying the house but I heard her go quiet. When I hung up, she didn't say anything. After that there was a lot of noise from the bedroom and when she came back into the room where I was sitting on the sofa she was wearing her coat.

I saw she was there, but I didn't look up. I just carried on reading the classifieds, working out how little I could send to get my mother a new TV set.

I heard the door slam. Then her footsteps on the wooden porch. Ducking under that hanging basket and on past the shaggy lawn. The owner of the house we rented had put the basket up before we moved in. For the first few weeks the fuschias, the pansies, the lobelia had greeted us. Their bright colors hung over us every time we turned the key in the lock. But I forgot to water them. It was my job, Iris said. She couldn't reach. Anyway, I forgot. The colors began to fade and soon the basket was dead and dry, rustling on windy days, nagging at me whenever I noticed.

I was sorry that I'd ignored Iris that morning, but I was waiting for her to leave so that I could plant up that old hanging basket again. I wanted to surprise her when she got back. After she'd let off steam at the mall. What could I say? I couldn't tell her what I was going to do, I'd told her too many times before what I was going to do and not done it. This time I thought I would use plants that didn't need so much care. The kind that could survive on a kind word now and then and little else. Heathers, ivy, maybe a cyclamen, I'd heard they thrived in dry conditions

I unhooked the hanging basket from the bracket beside the door and lifted it down. The plants had died so long ago, it was now just a basket of dust. There was a basket of dust hanging over the entrance to our house. Can you imagine.

I tipped the contents out onto the lawn. A cloud of dust flew up and a spider walked off under the porch. I took the basket to the faucet in the yard and washed it. It was made of wire coated with green plastic. In places the plastic had split and the wire had turned red with rust. Then I took a bag of compost and a tray of plants out of the car. I put them down on the step next to the basket. I lit a cigarette and sat on the step and read over the names of the plants. Someone had written the names out on little white sticks then stuck them into the pots. "Pelargonium", "Petunia." On one of the tags, "... *amelloides variegata*", the name was so long that part of it was hidden in the compost. Whether they were Greek or Latin the words were all new to me. Luckily the sales assistant at Plant Depot helped me to choose which ones would work best in a basket.

From a round mat made of coir I cut the liner and pressed it into the basket. At first the coir kept jumping up, so I made some cuts in it with a pair of scissors. Straight cuts from the edge towards the centre of the circle. Then I held it down while I poured a little earth onto the coir and it stayed in place. Around the basket's edge I made some holes in the liner through which the flowers could hang. Then I mixed a little slow release fertilizer into the compost and filled it level with the holes, ready to put in the pelargoniums. I wrapped their leaves in plastic so as not to damage them as I passed them through the cuts I'd made and then added more compost around their roots. It was important it was done right.

I don't remember using any fertilizer the last time. The plants were pretty much left to fend for themselves. The way my mother feels.

I lit another cigarette and opened a beer. For once I was in no hurry to get back to that sofa. I've spent a lot of time on that sofa since the plant closed. Iris says I practically live on that sofa. Then I put the lobelia around the edge, so that it would hang down and hide the rusty wire. I put in more compost around these too and left a space for the plant the clerk told me to put in the middle. He said it was a nice bushy plant with blue daisy-like flowers. I looked again at the tag marked "… *amelloides variegata*". *Felicia* it was called. Get that, Felicia. Iris had a little girl once called Felicia. It was before I knew her. I don't think she had her long, for a few hours I think she said. She doesn't even have a photograph.

The most important thing to remember with hanging baskets, the clerk said, was never to let the compost dry out. Once it dries out, he said, the plants aren't going to last long. He was right, too, that's what happened to the last one. I let the compost dry out. And then some. Iris says I should try drying out myself some time.

When the planting was done I hung the basket back on its bracket and went into the house to fetch water. The light was fading. My wife still wasn't home. While I waited for the can to fill up I looked about the kitchen. It took a while. There's some kind of problem with the water pressure, a bad valve, or something. Iris says if you want to take a bath on Thursday you'd better start drawing water on Monday. Anyway she's right, there's no water pressure. She'd really done a job on the place. It was tidy. Everything in its place, the way Iris likes it. Except for an envelope lying on the kitchen table. I left the can slowly filling under the faucet and I picked it up. My name was on the envelope. No address, just my name, in Iris's handwriting.

Growing Potatoes

with Bertolt Brecht

ARMAMENTS:
Spade
Fork

PROVISIONS:
Seed potatoes

POSITION:
Trench

ACT ONE

A garden somewhere in northern Europe. A soldier with the rank of SERGEANT stands, head bowed, at the foot of a bed of freshly tilled earth. In his left hand he holds his cap, in his right there is some soil. In the ground at the top of the bed there is a cross. As he drops a little of the soil onto the ground a woman, pushing a wheelbarrow, enters stage right. She is dressed in eclectic style: wellington boots, hat decorated with ferns, around her neck a fox stole. The wheelbarrow is filled with compost on top of which are piled all manner of garden tools. Beside her, dressed in clothes more suited to a child of five or six years of age, walks a teenage BOY. On his head the BOY wears an upturned hanging basket from which fronds of fern and grass protrude. He is attached to the handle of the wheelbarrow with a piece of gardening twine. On his shoulder he carries a rake. When she sees the SERGEANT, MOTHER COURAGE lets go of the handles and makes the BOY kneel out of sight behind the wheelbarrow from where he watches, the handle of his rake pointing upwards. Wiping her hands on her apron, she views the soldier with distrust. Finally she speaks.

MOTHER COURAGE. What do YOU want?

SERGEANT. (*Looking up from the ground. Placatory.*) Mother Courage, that's no way to address an old friend and an officer of the King's army. I see your bereavement was a recent one. No name yet on the cross. My condolences.

MOTHER COURAGE. I'm reserving it for you. That would put a smile on my face.

SERGEANT. (*Looking at the earth in his palm.*) I must compliment you on the quality of the grave. Full sun, good drainage, fertile soil, rich in organic matter. A pleasant spot indeed. Big man, was he?

MOTHER COURAGE. He was fifteen, and half starved. You ought to know.

SERGEANT. I only recruit them, what they make of army life is up to them. (*He sees MOTHER COURAGE and her son staring first down at the ground and then up at him.*)

MOTHER COURAGE. I brought him home from the battlefield in this wheelbarrow. He didn't weigh much more than a barrow of grass clippings.

SERGEANT. Well, you needn't look at me like that. I'm not in recruitment any more, I'm in procurement. You know what that means? The army's hungry, Mother Courage. There's a war on, and war requires vegetables.

MOTHER COURAGE. The army's good at making vegetables ... of other people's children.

SERGEANT. Now, now, Mother Courage, let's not be like that. Your sons brought glory to your name. (*The SERGEANT's attention turns now to a second patch of dug earth.*)

MOTHER COURAGE. Glory's not much use for making a soup. How's the Colonel? Eating well, is he?

SERGEANT. We're none of us eating well, Mother Courage. (*He looks around.*) Eighteen-inch paths between the beds. Beds no wider than five foot, paths on all sides. Would I be right in thinking ... This little plot has all the hallmarks of a well-planned vegetable garden. Are those potatoes over there?

MOTHER COURAGE. No, they're not. They're weeds.

SERGEANT. They don't look like weeds. My guess is this is your main crop, Mother C. What are they? Cara? Désirée? Pentland Squires? The boys love Pentland Squires. Too much to hope for a few Pink Fir Apples for the chef's salad, I suppose. What sort of weather have you been having?

MOTHER COURAGE. Shocking.

SERGEANT. Come, come now, in early September? Don't tell me you haven't had ninety to one hundred and forty days free of frost by now. More than enough for a healthy crop of spuds. Pests?

MOTHER COURAGE. Worst year ever. Cutworms, slugs,

potato cyst, eelworms, blackleg and violet root rot. It's a battlefield.

SERGEANT. That won't bother the regimental cook, he makes a lovely dish of violet root rot. Men love it. I'll take 'em.

MOTHER COURAGE. (*Screaming.*) Take my spuds? You might as well take the children, take us all. They're all we have to eat.

SERGEANT. Don't worry about feeding the children. The new recruiting officer will be along shortly, he'll be glad to take them off your hands.

MOTHER COURAGE. They're not ready.

SERGEANT. (*Looking now at MOTHER COURAGE's son peering over the wheelbarrow.*) Not ready? Look at him: no father, an empty belly and shaking like a leaf. I never saw a lad more suited to army life.

MOTHER COURAGE. Not him, the potatoes.

SERGEANT. Oh, them, I'm not worried about them. I know you, Mother Courage. No one drills a crop like you do. Drills dug three to six inches deep, spuds positioned fifteen inches apart, sprouts upward, am I right, Mother Courage? The stems well earthed-up to prevent any of your shallow crops from turning green in the sunlight, a light layer of straw to cover them on frosty nights. There's not a soul round here knows how to take care of their spuds like you. Pass me that fork. (*The two of them fight over the fork. The SERGEANT wins, pushing MOTHER COURAGE to the ground.*)

MOTHER COURAGE. (*Screaming.*) You can't just dig them up. You need to cut the stems down first, then you leave the potatoes in the ground for another two weeks.

SERGEANT. Two weeks? What's the point of that? My men
  need feeding now.

MOTHER COURAGE. To harden the skins, you callous bastard. They'll be too tender, The shock of lifting them
  would be too much.

SERGEANT. The army? Wait? The army is hungry.

MOTHER COURAGE. The army's always hungry. And the
  army can never wait. Why does it have to keep picking my
  fruit to feed it? Oh, my poor boy that you took and never
  brought home to me. Why don't you just piss off and die
  for a change. (*She sings. The BOY, his head just peering over
  the edge of the wheelbarrow, takes up a trowel and begins beating time on a spade.*)

They mowed him down.
they peeled his skin,
they mashed his flesh
and then they dug him in.

Oh, the army
plants our boys in trenches,
fertilised with glory in the mud,
an early crop, that never quenches
the war's appetite for blood.

Boys who once were,
the apples of our eyes
are now a crop rotting in the ground,
unharvested though not forgotten,
fed and watered with politicians' lies.

They mowed him down,
they peeled his skin,
they mashed his flesh
and then they dug him in.

(*Singing mournfully now.*)
I dug him out,
with a hoe and a prayer,
I kissed his cheek
but his cheek wasn't there.

SERGEANT. He keeps good time, that boy of yours. We need a new drummer boy. The last one had his arm taken off by a cannonball. The troops don't follow him like they used to. Wouldn't you like to be a little drummer boy? (*THE SERGEANT bends down towards the BOY and holds out a coin. As the BOY reaches to take it MOTHER COURAGE hits him across the knuckles with a trowel.*)

MOTHER COURAGE. He's not old enough.

SERGEANT. He looks old enough. How old are you, boy? Wouldn't you like to wear a coat of red and gold?

MOTHER COURAGE. Coat of what? Dead and cold you mean? Hang it on somebody else's child.

SERGEANT. Now, now, Mother Courage, let the boy speak for himself.

MOTHER COURAGE. He can't speak. I learnt my lesson after you took the last one. I never want any of my children to speak again.

SERGEANT. What do you mean?

MOTHER COURAGE. He knows what's best for him.

SERGEANT. All right, all right, the boy's none of my business, let's see what your potatoes have to say for themselves.

MOTHER COURAGE. Can't you even wait for a cloudy day? I wouldn't lift them in this light, they'll turn green in an hour.

SERGEANT. A dry, sunny day like this? Perfect conditions for harvesting potatoes. I'll soon have them out of the sun.

(Barking aloud the commands of a military drill, the SERGEANT uses the fork to present arms then, with a shout, as though he is making a bayonet charge, he begins driving the fork into the ground. Almost immediately a handful of potatoes is turned up.)

SERGEANT. Look at those beauties, Mother Courage. A few good thrusts from a soldier and Mother Earth soon spills up her guts. (*MOTHER COURAGE has pulled her son close and together the two watch as the SERGEANT continues stabbing ferociously at the ground. When he stops the bed is devastated. All around him, potatoes lie on the surface of the ground. The SERGEANT wipes the sweat from his brow, and looks back now at the bed marked by the cross.*) You wouldn't be hiding a crop there under the unknown soldier, would you, Mother C? (*MOTHER COURAGE clings tighter to her son, her face defiant.*) You'd be surprised at how many filthy peasants I've known cut all the foliage off a crop at the first sight of a soldier. What are you nurturing under here, Mother C? Nothing that a good prod with a garden fork won't uncover. (*The SERGEANT now takes up the fork and repeats the drill. Then he begins digging the fork into the bed marked with the cross.*

MOTHER COURAGE wails. He uncovers something and falls to his knees in the mud and begins digging with his hands in the dirt.) What's this? Looks like parsnips ... I knew it. You're a crafty old bitch, Mother C. Just for that I've changed my mind. I'm not even leaving you a handful of spuds for tonight's soup.

(The SERGEANT struggles now, pulling excitedly at the long white growths he has uncovered. As the bed is despoiled MOTHER COURAGE and her son grow increasingly troubled. When, after one last heave, the ground gives up its hold, the SERGEANT falls back, horrified, to see that he has been pulling on the skeletal fingers of a corpse. At the same time the BOY screams, a high, long, unbroken sound. Protruding from the ground we now see an arm. Clad in the filthy red and gold of a military dress coat, it is bent in such a way that it appears to be giving a salute. On seeing this mark of respect, the SERGEANT rises to his feet and, standing to attention, returns the salute. As he does so, the BOY resumes his drumming. This time the rhythm is that of Holst's 'Mars, Bringer of War'.)

Curtain

Dividing Bamboo

with Isabel Allende

TOOLS:
Fork
Saw
Spade
Faith

For two decades the treasure of Sergio de Flores had lain undisturbed. Its hiding place had been marked with a single cane of bamboo planted by the great bank robber himself. That cane had now become a clump whose ebony culms could be heard on windy days, whispering his name after dusk.

When Claveles came upon him one night, taking refuge in her garden, Sergio had begged her not to give him up to the police. And while she stared in wonder at his thick lips and heavy brow, he told her of the robbery he had carried out that very day and how, cornered by the police, he had buried its proceeds in the east bed of her modest garden. Before he left the following morning, he separated the cane from the potted bamboo on the terrace and planted it in the ground that covered his sunken treasure and swore he would love her till the end of his days. She, in turn, had sworn never to dig up the bed and never to ask him about its contents. And vowed to herself to water the single stem every day in honour of the mysterious lover whose return she awaited with a burning passion.

Their courtship was short. His proposal, made unexpectedly as Claveles helped him escape from the window of a ladies' convenience, was accepted with a heart overflowing with joy. The events of their wedding day were indicative of the relationship that was to follow. On hearing that a photographer from the local newspaper had arrived at the reception, Sergio declared himself overtaken by a sudden fever. While the bride, seated on a cloud of white organza, smiled stoically at the camera, her groom fled across the lawn on a stolen bicycle, pursued by a young man dressed in the uniform of the city telegraph office. She did not see the groom again until six days later, when he arrived early one morning having exchanged his Sunday best for a bunch of peonies, a false beard and a suit of green serge.

Supported by an unshakeable faith, Claveles grew accustomed to the sudden departures of her husband, persuading herself that his frequent absences and the impassioned partings that preceded them held a tragic romance that kept their love new and the passion of their youth evergreen. Once, in the spring of the fifth year of their marriage, her husband was gone for three months. Dispirited by his long absence, Claveles sought comfort in the now densely crowded patch of bamboo. With saw and secateurs she cut away its dead and damaged culms, clearing room for light and air, until only the youngest, most intensely coloured canes remained. By the eightieth day of their separation these tender cares had turned to obsession. When finally he returned Sergio found his wife half crazed with mourning. With ash-smeared cheeks, dressed in her wedding gown dyed black, Claveles was standing in the moonlit garden, humming to herself as she polished the remaining canes until they shone like jet. From that day on, frightened by such a spectacular display of grief, Sergio kept his absences shorter.

Together the couple lived a frugal life. Claveles' modest income, unsupplemented due to her spouse's reluctance to take a job, soon found itself stretched by the demands of his outlaw life. Whenever Claveles grew tired of their meagre existence and questioned why they should deny themselves the fruits of her husband's life of crime he laughed at her simplicity. The police, he would say, were waiting for just such an oversight. His success in avoiding prison lay, he claimed, in his refusal to spend a single peso of his daringly acquired fortune and in his readiness, at any moment, to leave the comforts of his home for the open road. This he did frequently. On feast days and festivals it was her husband's custom to arrive late or leave early and he formed a habit of fleeing the house before noon on Christmas Day, claiming the police would call for him on just such a festival expecting to find him at his home.

These often unpredictable absences did nothing to diminish Claveles' unalterable devotion. When she begged him to take her with him his refusals were stern, his severity tempered by the passion of his goodbyes and his descriptions of a shining future in which she would wear dresses and jewels fit for a queen, and they would live every day together on a galleon moored in the rolling canopy of the rainforest.

Between them they invented a secret language of signs that would alert him if ever the police were to set a trap for his return. The hips left on a climbing rose to tell him that sharp shooters were lying in wait on the rooftop; runner beans trained into a cross of St Andrew as a sign that a patrol lay in the potting shed; the water lilies turned upside down on the surface of the pond, a signal that the captain and his guard were holding Claveles prisoner in the house. None of these scenarios ever came to pass but Claveles rejoiced in these and a hundred other subterfuges, revelling in the fantasy that each time her lover came to her he risked his life to share her bed.

In the last month of his life, Sergio de Flores succumbed to a fever of the brain. When, for the first time, Claveles saw her handsome bandit listen without alarm to the sound of steps approaching their door, she knew then that his sickness was grave. For twenty-eight days the fever raged, and while the bank robber gave voice to the ravings of his demented mind, and spoke of treasures lost and loved ones left behind, Claveles, blissfully, wiped the sweat from the muscled contours of his body. The period of his sickness was by far the longest time Claveles had spent in the company of her husband. And as she held a sponge soaked in honeyed water to his parched lips she gave thanks to God for the fever that kept him by her side, cherishing every moment spent enveloped in the sharp aroma of his sweat. Only when the affliction spread to his heart did her gratitude diminish and her prayers for his recovery begin in earnest. But by then it was too late. At its peak the fever grew so intense and Sergio's temperature so high that Claveles smelt the hair singe on her head as she lay against his burning cheek. When finally his temperature subsided it was not because the fever had broken; rather that it had consumed him, as a forest fire burns until there is no more to burn and de Flores, cradled in the blistered arms of his wife, breathed his last and died.

Half crazed with grief and remorse, Claveles took a spade and, as her husband's body lay cooling, she walked out into the garden. Unmindful any more of the promises she had made, or of the warnings she had been given, she made her way to the tall thicket of black canes, and there, like a fighter making a mark in the sand, she took the broad blade and drew a line in the ground.

Years of neglect had packed the soil about the bamboo as hard as granite so that breaking even its surface was a struggle. Stepping on and off the spade as she struggled to make headway she felt the sweat trickle down between her breasts, making her cotton blouse stick to her still elegant figure, but the blade did not budge.

So consumed was she by her battle with the earth, she did not notice the young passer-by who had stopped to watch her work. Intrigued by the delicate woman balanced on the stationary blade like a trapeze artist on a wire, the young onlooker watched until finally the impatience of one who goes unnoticed prompted him to speak. "Can I help?" he asked.

Though the voice of the stranger was gentle, there was a familiarity to his features that at once unsettled her. Through long years spent listening to the cautions of her husband Claveles had grown secretive. Warily she watched him raise his foot to rest it on the fence. Then, ignoring his question, she looked back at the ground, ruefully surveying the minor cuts and scratches produced by her exertions with the spade. She looked back at the questioner and this time saw how tightly the fabric of his trouser hugged his thigh. His leg was heavy and the ground, as she had discovered, was very hard.

"I am trying to lift this bamboo. But the ground here is packed solid and I am so slight."

Requiring no more invitation, the chivalrous onlooker leapt the fence and, offering his hand as he bowed, waited for Claveles to step from the spade as though he were helping a countess from her carriage. Accepting his offer Claveles stepped from the spade and watched in awe as now, in the young man's hands, its unremitting blade began to cut through the earth like the hull of a boat through water.

Rejoicing in the unexpected opportunity to display his strength, the handsome digger stole surreptitious glances at the tearful gardener by his side, hoping for a sign of admiration and so beguiled by her tears that eventually he asked, "Does this plant mean something special?"

"My husband planted it."

"You're fortunate to have a gardener for a husband. My father has never gardened once in his life."

"It is the only thing he ever planted in this garden," she said and with her sleeve she wiped the tears from her cheeks and smiled. "I met him here, on this very spot. He was standing there where you are standing now. And I loved him from the first."

"Does he know you are digging it up?"

"My husband is dead."

She waited for him to speak, but the stranger only bowed

his head and resumed digging; only once, when a root resisted, did she hear the hoarse panting of his breath, sounding as though it came from far away, and her body began again to shake with silent weeping.

When the clump was nearly free she became anxious about uncovering the treasure whose secret she had kept for so many years, and she thanked him for his work and gestured him away. But the root ball, when she tried to lift it, was much heavier than she expected. Seeing her struggle the young man stepped forward again, and together the two of them began to lift the shallow rooted plant until, with a wrenching sound, it came free, like a city bristling with skyscrapers leaving in its wake a crater in which only dust could be seen. In vain Claveles ran her fingers over the earth searching for the lid of a strongbox, the decaying canvas of a bag of coin, and finding only dust.

"What is your name?" she said.

"Sergio." At his reply a shiver went down Claveles' spine.

"Sergio, the hole is not deep enough. Dig deeper. I will pay you for your trouble."

On her knees now, Claveles crouched over the deepening hole, her hands clutched together as if in prayer while the young man kept digging.

With each cut the hole grew deeper and the digger grew more concerned for the tragic creature, muttering strange incantations into the growing void. When the hole was nearly four feet deep, and as wide again, she told him to stop. Her arms wrapped about her slender body, her attention turned again to the clump of soil that held the knot of black canes. "Cut it in two. Cut the root ball in half."

When it became apparent that the cluster of roots had grown too dense to be cut easily with a spade, Claveles fetched a saw. She watched the hypnotic movement of his muscular arm as the newcomer knelt beside her and began to cut through the knot of roots that held together the tall canes of bamboo. When the clump was nearly divided he put down the saw and with only his hands began pulling apart the last of the soil, carefully trying to keep as many as possible of the young shoots intact. In that moment, thinking she saw a glimpse of something gold, the desperate widow clutched at the lump of earth, clawing and picking at the roots.

"Take care," said the good Samaritan, snatching the roots out of her reach. "If we are replanting we should keep as much earth as possible attached to the roots." But overcome with fear and impatience, Claveles, seeing not so much as a single peso fall from the dense mass of rhizomes, no longer cared.

"Cut again," she said. Soon the two clumps of bamboo had become four. Still not a grain of gold or silver could be seen. Again and again Claveles gave the order to cut until the garden was strewn with the black canes that lay about their feet like a morbid calligraphy, their message decipherable only to Claveles, who now began again to sob pitifully. "The doctors have taken the last of my money. My husband lies still on his deathbed and I have not a penny to pay for him to be buried."

"Your husband is not yet buried?" Sergio looked down at the hole he had dug. "Where is he, then?"

The question seemed to startle the bereaved woman, who suddenly leapt to her feet and, with hands black with earth, ran from the garden and into the house.

When finally the young man grew tired of waiting he

followed her. When he found her she was slumped on the floor in the bedroom. Beside her on the bed, his face and body smeared with dark patches of earth left by the distraught hands of his kneeling wife, lay the body of Sergio de Flores. Claveles appeared calm now. Seeing the stranger pause respectfully in the doorway, her heart went out to the young man, who could not have expected such a scene to follow his act of kindness. His wide eyes filled with tears. Then with a shout the visitor ran forward, uttered the name of his father and fell sobbing across the body of the dead man.

Confused by the stranger's extraordinary outburst Claveles was at first slow to understand. Then she looked more closely at the young face, twisted in grief, and at the thick lips and heavy brow of her dead husband. Slowly a picture began to form. For the first time Claveles began to understand the nature of the half-life she had lived with Sergio de Flores, and the mystery of the half she did not know. And grief swept down on her in a new guise.

When the first shock of their shared grief had passed, the two survivors began to talk. The son told how, when his father had not returned home, inspired by a dream, his mother had sent him to look among the narrow streets and gardens for which Claveles' neighbourhood was well known. Together they remembered Sergio's wandering and invasive habits and the difficulties of containing this most expansive of characters.

Between them they carried the deceased to the hole left where the bamboo had once grown. There, with the dead man's knees touching his chin, they arranged the body in the position of the last rest. When his son remarked that there was scarcely a foot of space between his father's head and the surface of the ground his widow's answer was clear. "For a man like him it is enough," said Claveles. "He knows how to keep his head down."

After he had shovelled home the last of the soil the younger Sergio collected two of the black canes from the ground, still with part of the root ball attached. "Shouldn't we make a cross?" he said.

"I have a better idea," said Claveles and, taking one of the black rods from his hand, she made an ample hole in the freshly dug ground at the edge of the grave. Dousing it well with water, she planted the rod alongside the grave; then she planted another, and so on, until all of the canes had been used up and their dark stems rose up about the grave like the bars of a cage. Together then, the deceased's wife and child joined their hands in prayer, and standing before the dark bars of his prison, whose walls would continue to grow ever higher, the two mourners offered a prayer for the soul of Sergio de Flores, a divided man perhaps, but one capable of putting down roots almost anywhere.

On the Art of Mowing

with Niccolò Machiavelli

INSTRUMENTS:
Scythe
Shears
Poison
Implacable resolution

All gardens consist of three basic habitats: the flower bed, the mixed border and the lawn laid to grass. Of these I say at once that there are more difficulties in preserving a lawn than in the upkeep of any other. The varied character and diversity of a flower bed demands a degree of freedom such that could not be tolerated in a lawn. This freedom is extended further still in the mixed border wherein a multitude of species are permitted to cohabit with a more or less self-regulating pattern. Such behaviour may well be compared with that in republics or in the farthest outposts of a ruler's dominion, in which, by virtue of their distance from the capital, subjects exist in a state of near anarchy. How different then is the lawn, the capital, so to speak, of a gardener's territory, his court even, in which his talent is put under the closest examination and where unrest and treachery do most to threaten his government.

Therefore I say that a lawn keeper, between the months of March and October, ought to have no other aim or thought, nor select anything else for his study, than the art of frequent mowing and its rules and discipline. Regular mowing not only punishes delinquent plants but also contains the ambitions of those grasses and weeds who through rapid advancement seek to obtain prominence amongst their fellows. In this way a wise gardener is able to ensure the vigour of his grasses without permitting them to grow so great in stature as to present a challenge to his authority.

Frequency of mowing alone does not make for good government. The severity of the cut will also decide the success or failure of a gardener's rule. The gardener who shows himself too clement and sets his scythe to cut above one and one half inches serves only to encourage the coarse grasses to swamp the finer. By the latter I refer to the bents, fescue and timothy, all loyal grasses recognised as worthy inhabitants of the ideal lawn and yet known to have been overrun on many occasions by the barbarian invader. If, on the contrary, a gardener seeks to give a show of strength and sets his scythe to cut shorter than one quarter of an inch, he risks weakening the grass; he places its roots in danger of starvation, and the natural impoverishment that is the consequence of starved roots disadvantages the lawn as a whole. Of all gardeners it is most difficult for the new gardener to avoid the imputation of cruelty. His dominion is so menaced by dangers of every sort: docks and sorrels; creeping buttercups; crowsfoot; the greater plantain and its hoary relation, ribwort; starweed; clover; white lesser trefoil; bird's foot trefoil; black medick; dandelion; cat's ear; daisies and pearlwort, that if he is not possessed of genius or ability, violence may be his only course.

The rule in mowing is indeed little and often. The Duke of Milan, who cuts twice a week in summer when the grass is growing vigorously, by applying a moderate force frequently, finds his subjects are reassured and readily accept his rule. The gardener who does otherwise, such as the Duke de Sforza, who mowed less often but with greater severity, in causing a sudden loss of such a large quantity of leaf in his subjects, only encouraged the treacheries and invasion of the outside mosses and weeds that were his downfall.

Moss in itself is of course not the primary cause of run-down turf; it is rather a symptom of other weaknesses in a gardener's mastery of his dominion. Underfeeding, water-logging and even failure to water during drought are all possible causes of moss invasion and until these are tackled the use of mercenaries such as moss killer will not return a lawn to good health, but will remain a constant drain on the resources of a ruler.

When dealing with threats and invasions of this sort the rule is not little and often but to be cruel and excessive. There are of course those, such as the Duke of Urbino, who preach tolerance of moss and consider its bright colour and spongy texture merits worthy of inclusion in a lawn. I say that moss is the worst of treacheries, requiring a gardener to uproot it with the utmost severity.

Many gardeners are slow to react to the appearance of other apparently friendly threats such as daisies or pearlwort, both of which have shown themselves capable of spreading quickly and destroying large areas of grass in a relatively short period of time. The most effective check to their advance was demonstrated by Prince Cesare Borgia when in one single application of poison he successfully cleared the gardens of Castel Sant'Angelo of all the daisies in whom he saw an immediate threat to his authority. Nor do I doubt he would have hesitated to repeat this or any crueller treatment to be sure of eradicating other threats to his power.

The prince was fortunate in that daisies and mosses are not difficult to identify, but there are other less visible threats of which a gardener must beware if he is to govern well. Certain species of native and natural grasses, if inadequately suppressed when their land was originally taken from them, are distinctly undesirable. First among these are the coarse-leaved grasses: Yorkshire fog, cocksfoot, creeping soft grass and wall barley grass, all capable of forming unsightly clumps in closely mown turf, and the gardener that counts them among his citizens may never be sure that his lawn is entirely under his control.

A lawn that has been left for too long to live by its own rules ceases to be a lawn. It becomes instead a place of savagery, in which rivalling factions compete for territory, until the weak are overwhelmed by the strong. A gardener who finds himself in possession of such a territory, whether through fortune, inheritance or sloth, will certainly lose the respect of both and, unless he is willing to enter into a long campaign, has only one course of action before him. First he must drive out the troublemakers, by uprooting the lawn entirely, then, to avoid a recurrence of the uprising, the rebels and their descendants must be burnt and their ashes scattered on the ground. Only then will it be safe to repopulate his territory with more governable subjects. This he may do in two ways: either by seeding the cleared land or, if his fortune is sufficient, by the acquisition of rolls of turf. Neither path is straightforward; the sower of seed contends with the raids of birds and other thieves hungry for grain while the layer of turf must take pains to support the new settlers with provisions until such time as his colonists are established. In short there is nothing more difficult to take in hand, more perilous to conduct or more uncertain of its success than the laying of a new lawn.

May the troubles of all who embark on such an undertaking serve as a warning to those gardeners who, neglecting the art of mowing, think more often of ease than of shears. The successful lawn keeper is never idle. He is master of his art and always undertakes his treatments before a problem arises. In this way troubles are kept at bay and his lawn remains an object of admiration to his neighbours.

Planting a Fruit Tree

with Henrik Ibsen

PROPS:
Spade
Compost
Hole

ACT I

A garden. A grassy outcrop. About it a gloomy fjord landscape shrouded in steady rain. At the top of the garden, half concealed behind a small copse of trees, smoke rises from a chimney, beneath it an attractive house with a conservatory. On the lawn is JULIA, a woman in her early thirties elegantly dressed in outdoor clothes. Her hat, pushed back off her head, hangs on her back. Her wet hair sticks to her forehead. She is perspiring and short of breath. In her hands she holds a spade. Centre stage, a hole.

Beside the hole, in a pot there is an apple tree. With her free hand JULIA removes her hat and hands it to HELDER, a man in his late thirties, of sickly complexion. HELDER is sitting in a bath chair; his right leg, extended straight in front of him, is heavily strapped. He wears a dark overcoat, over his shoulders and legs are rugs, and on his head he wears a hat with a wide brim over which he is holding an umbrella. He is smoking a cigar.

JULIA. Is *this* deep enough? Can't we plant the tree now?

HELDER. Now what did I say, my little skylark? The hole needs to be at least three times the size of the pot. There you go again, my pet, always trying to take short cuts.

JULIA. (*Pouting.*) The hole looks quite deep enough to me. Oh, Helder, it's quite a bore digging such a big hole for such a tiny tree.

HELDER. When it comes to digging holes the rule is simple. The bigger, the better. It also needs to be one and a half times the depth of the root ball. Come on, my little squirrel, one last effort and it will be done. Now you're quite sure that the root ball has been given a good soaking?

JULIA. Oh yes, Helder, I left it soaking this morning, at the edge of the pond. When I went back the pot had become so heavy I nearly fell in trying to get it out. I had to ask Gunther to help me in the end.

HELDER. Dear old Gunther. It's good to have him back round the place. The hole's looking good. Now if you pick up that fork you can use it to scarify the sides.

JULIA. Whatify? Honestly, Helder, I've no idea what you're talking about.

HELDER. Scarify. If we want our roots to be able to spread, we don't want the earth at the edges of the hole to be too tightly packed, do we? Use the fork to soften it up a bit. There's a good girl. Dear old Gunther seems to have taken quite a shine to our Oswald since he got back; he was carrying the boy on his shoulders when I passed them coming back from the village the other day. (*From off stage the sound of a child's voice shouting 'Charge!' HELDER and JULIA, who is now standing in the hole, both pause and look towards the sound. With joy on their faces the couple watch as their son, OSWALD, a rosy-cheeked young boy in a green sweater, runs past shouting with joy and exits stage right. JULIA's expression quickly changes to one of worry.*)

HELDER. (*Still looking towards OSWALD's exit.*) How he does love to play with the gardener's son. It's hard to keep them apart these days. I suppose it's all right for now, but it won't do when he's older. Say, have you ever noticed, my little squirrel, how alike those two boys are?

JULIA. (*Uttering a cry, then, trying to disguise its cause, she quickly puts a finger in her mouth and sucks on an imaginary injury.*)

HELDER. What is it?

JULIA. (*Taking the finger from her mouth and examining it*) All boys their age are alike, Helder.

HELDER: Yes, I suppose you're right, my little skylark. (*HELDER takes a puff on his cigar and watches JULIA struggling in the heavy soil.*) Old Gunther certainly seems to be encouraging the friendship. Quite unlike his wife. (*Off stage, the occasional shout of boys at play is heard. JULIA looks at HELDER, then kneels down beside the hole and reaches in to pull out a handful of earth.*)

JULIA. (*Her voice appearing from the hole.*) What do you mean?

HELDER. Don't you remember when Frau Gunther gave poor Oswald that terrible slap last summer? When she found him eating raspberries in the fruit patch. The boy's kept his distance from her ever since. She's not that nice even to you, I've noticed.

JULIA. (*Straining to reach into the hole and to remove the last of the loose soil.*) She's nice enough. Tell me, Helder, your little squirrel is quite lost now, can I take the tree out of its pot yet?

HELDER. There you go again. Such an impatient little skylark. Always trying to rush to the fun part and never paying any mind to good preparation. You remember what happened when you insisted on decorating the Christmas tree last year before it was properly weighted in the pot?

JULIA. Yes, Helder, you're right. Sometimes your little skylark has no patience at all.

HELDER. You need to mix the soil you've taken out of the hole with all that lovely rich compost in the wheelbarrow there. Imagine you're mixing the ingredients for a cake. (*Using the spade, JULIA lifts some of the compost onto the mound of soil on the ground and then stirs it with the garden fork.*)

JULIA. (*Playfully.*) Aren't you glad, Helder, that your little Julia doesn't really make cakes like this? (*Looking up, she sees Helder is again looking towards the children at play. From her pocket she takes a paper bag and quickly pops a macaroon into her mouth. She tucks the bag out of sight then, pretending to be in a sulk ...*) Helder, you're not watching what I'm doing. Very well, I'm going to take the tree out of its pot.

HELDER. You can, nearly, just as soon as you've put some of that cake mix into the bottom of the hole. That's it, a little more perhaps, let's make a nice little cushion for our apple tree to sit on. Now you can take the tree out of its pot. Lay it on its side first. Then you can pull the pot away from the tree ... (*As JULIA crouches over the pot the bag of macaroons falls from her pocket.*) What's this? Has my little poppet been spending money again at the sweet shop? (*Guiltily JULIA shakes her head, then slides the pot away from the root ball and we see the earth, still holding together in the shape of the pot.*)

JULIA. Oh look, Helder. There at the base of the trunk. The tree has had a nasty misshapen ankle, just like you.

HELDER. Don't think you'll distract me from your little secrets so easily. Hand them over. (HELDER *holds out his hand. With a great show of mock guilt and shyness, JULIA approaches HELDER and hands over the paper bag.*)

JULIA. If your skylark promises not to do it again, could you forgive her?

HELDER. (*Won over by JULIA's act.*) I suppose I could. If she kept her promise not to do it again.

(*JULIA kneels and takes one of the macaroons from the confiscated bag. With one hand she removes the cigar from HELDER's mouth and with the other she places a macaroon between his lips.*)

JULIA. (*Making eyes.*) Could you forgive her anything? If she promised not to do it again?

HELDER. Anything? ... I'm not sure about anything. (*Looking up at HELDER, JULIA begins to make little whining sounds like a puppy.*) Well, I suppose I could. (*Sterner*) If I thought she'd learnt her lesson ... and could keep her promise not to do it again. (*JULIA springs up to her feet and hugs HELDER. Then she returns to the tree by the hole.*) And that swelling at the base of the trunk, it's not an injury, it's where the cultivar has been grafted onto the rootstock. Oh, there's so much my pretty little squirrel doesn't know, isn't there?

JULIA. Cultivars? Rootstocks? I'm sure I have no idea what you're talking about.

HELDER. Most fruit trees are grown onto a rootstock, usually taken from some sturdy variety that knows how to take care of itself. As for the cultivar, well, that could be any variety chosen for the beauty of its flowers or the quality of its fruit. That's it, tease some of the roots out from the root ball so that they don't carry on growing around in a circle.

JULIA. (*Carefully pulling the roots out so as to keep as much soil as possible around them.*) Isn't it wrong to grow one plant on the roots of another?

HELDER. Not at all. If the rootstock is a better provider of food and water, or better suited to the land in which the cultivar is to be grown, then why not? If giving a tree the best possible chance of success means doing it on roots that have proven themselves fittest for the job, then that's what we should do. You can put it in the hole now. Keep it nice and straight.

JULIA. What would Pastor Manders think?

HELDER. Exactly the same thing, I think. Why, at the vicarage he has a whole orchard grown on exactly the same principle. That's it, you can begin filling the hole now with your cake mix.

(*At first JULIA holds the tree straight, then as more soil is added it stands upright by itself, and she adds the rest of the soil and compost mix.*)

HELDER. Now tread the soil down with your foot to make sure the tree is properly anchored in the ground. (*Looking up.*) I swear this rain is getting worse. It's good for the tree, but we'll have to get you in by the fire, my bedraggled little squirrel. Come along.

(*JULIA lays the spade across HELDER's lap. By now the wheels of the chair have sunk into the lawn and JULIA makes heavy work of pushing HELDER back in the direction of the house. The couple moves up stage, fading into the rain and mist. In the distance the silhouette of a man with a boy on his shoulders can just be made out. When JULIA sees it, she pauses and begins to adjust the rug on HELDER'S legs.*)

JULIA. I know you will forgive me, but before I go to the fire, Helder, I have something to tell you.

Curtain

Removing a Sucker

with Bret Easton Ellis

TOOLS:
Hunter wellington boots in classic green
Gold Leaf Tough Touch gloves
Sneeboer hoe
Felco Professional Model 7 secateurs

I'm wearing a four-button Sea Island cotton shirt in citrine from Saks, moleskin trousers in Ohio green by Ralph Lauren with a Mulberry belt in tan leather, when I step out onto the roof garden of my apartment on the Upper West Side. Panning over the mixed border the bright sap-green stem catches my eye. It seems cleaner, more vibrant than its neighbours, an emerald green diagonal nearly six feet long.

My fingers move now to my hip, and as my green Hunter wellies step onto the buoyant sward of the artificial lawn, I pull the Felco Professional Model 7 secateurs from their holster. The Felco no. 7 is a superbly designed ergonomic bypass secateur aimed at the professional. It has a rotating handle that revolves on its axis, allowing the fingers to move naturally, reducing the blisters and hand fatigue that can accompany prolonged pruning. Its unique swivel action requires up to thirty per cent less effort than conventional models and offers maximum comfort. The swivelling handle took some getting used to at first, but now I wonder how I ever lived without it. Neither the cutting nor the anvil blades are riveted, so they are easy to replace and their narrow, pointed design allows for exceptionally close cutting. It's hard to appreciate all its benefits on the first cut, but believe me, this is the ultimate secateur and you'll want to savor its qualities over time.

How the fuck did this thing grow so big? So fast? Up close I count the number of leaves in each cluster ... There are seven of them. Not five, but seven. They're paler, too, and the thorns are a different shape to those on the main plant. It's a parasite, a waster, a bum, panhandling life and energy away from the cultivar from whose rootstock it's sprung. It's a sucker.

In this garden alone there are so many parasites I can no longer keep count. Aphids, caterpillars, mealy bugs, red mite, whitefly, slugs, snails, mildew, mould, rust, scab, wilt, tulip fire, bud blast, canker and squirrel. Fucking squirrel. Bulb-eating, fruit-stealing, nut-burying fucking squirrel. All this in one tiny urban patch of green. The last year alone this garden has known more toxic liabilities than a fucking Wall Street bank.

I put the secateurs back into the holster. Cutting it back isn't going to work, to this kind of sucker that's just more stimulation to grow. Pretty soon I'll be overrun with the suckers. No, I am going to rip it off, with my bare hands.

Correction: I'm wearing Tough Touch gloves by Gold Leaf. After the manicure I had yesterday I'm fairly confident they'll keep out anything the garden might throw my way. I press down on the sucker's stem, watching as it springs back, vibrating, more elastic and flexible than the darker old wood of the cultivar. I trace along its length until I reach the spot where it disappears beneath the freshly tilled earth. One of those dumb fuck Mexicans poking around aimlessly with his hoe must have caused it. A small nick in the rootstock, that's all it takes, one little jab in the dark and next thing you know another sucker is born.

Holding the cherry-wood handle of a Sneeboer hand hoe I begin pulling earth away from the base of the plant, digging the last part with my hands until I have exposed the place where the sucker emerges from the rootstock. With my thumb and forefinger I take hold of one of its thorns and bend it back. When it snaps away from the stem it leaves behind a little ellipse-shaped wound of raw white flesh. It is pathetic how easily the sucker is stripped of its defences. I break off another and another. When I grow bored with breaking off the thorns I wrap both hands around the defenceless stem and squeezing tightly I wrench the sucker away from the root. There is a pop, then the sound of fibres tearing, epidermis, cortex, cambium splitting away from the root and finally, as the sucker comes away in my hands, taking with it any dormant buds that might still be lurking at its base, green-white sap splatters my face and arms and I fall back through the foliage onto the Canadian cedar decking. I look at the white sap dripping from the stump, spilling like semen onto the soil. Beside myself, I press my tongue into the open wound. At the taste of the bitter juice I begin biting on the end of the amputated stem, tearing off strips of skin, shoving it into my mouth, choking on the taste of chlorophyll and cellulose and I cast the mangled sucker onto the lawn where it lies like a green length of intestine while I, happy to be burying the last traces of one more fucking parasite, begin filling the earth back around the rootstock.

From an open door comes the sound of a television, the theme tune to *Wheel of Fortune*. My shirt stained with earth and sap, I stand up among the flowers to look over the fence for the source of the music. On the other side, a copy of this month's *Vanity Fair* by her side, is a hardbody, sunbathing. She's pretty, too. She's wearing a green bikini with sequinned bra and jewelled briefs from Max Mara and matching green sandals from Sergio Rossi. Seeing me, she moves her weight onto her elbow and with her free hand raises her Persol sunglasses. "What's that on your face?" she says. I remove the gloves. My face is wet and sticky with xylem and phloem, sap and slime stain my cheeks and smear the lenses of my Wayfarer sunglasses. Then, as she watches, with my fingers I take hold of the nearest rose, spreading its petals like the multiple lips of a too heavily made-up mouth, and sniff, inhaling its perfume. I slide my left hand down beneath its sepals and squeezing tightly I slash at its stem with the secateurs. The stem is half severed, I can feel the rose clinging on by a few stringy threads, struggling pointlessly. This time I place the blades around the stem and hissing I squeeze the hand grips close until with a soft crunch sound the rose comes away in my hand leaving its ragged stump pointing stupidly up in the sky. As I hold the severed bloom out over the fence, its petals shaking spasmodically, I can smell the scent of chlorophyll, I can feel the crushed wet stem cold on my hand.

"I want you to have this," I say. "Haven't I seen you at Daisy's?" She sits up on the teak and chrome lounger, sips from her Coke with a straw and I notice now how well endowed she is behind the sequins. She looks at the cut flower, my winning smile, the tanned muscles of my arm, the smeared black lenses of my Wayfarers. There's an awkward silence as I wipe the blades clean on top of the fence and then I say, "I've got a rather expensive bottle of Pouilly-Fuissé chilling in the house."

Finally she smiles. "I don't know Daisy," she says. "My name's Rosa."

Burying Bulbs in Autumn

with Sylvia Plath

TOOLS:
Bulbs
Trowel
Earth
Light
Darkness

I swallowed trying again to clear the bitter taste from my mouth then I tipped the bulbs from the bag and watched as their fat little bodies rolled around on the garden path. Bulbs with purple skin the texture of old oil paintings, pale anaemic bulbs trailing coarse tufts of root from their bodies, fat-bottomed bulbs covered from head to toe in maternity gowns that disintegrated at the touch, they all bounced and scuttled on the ground, for a moment like beetles startled to be caught in the light.

The dumpy little tubers, too dumb to think, then grew still, waiting to be put into the beds in which they would give birth to the offspring, now coiled like springs in their fat round bellies.

Daffodil or hyacinth? Tulip or snowdrop? I couldn't tell, so I separated the bulbs into groups according to their size. With the trowel I slit open the ground and cut a hole. The hole I made three times deeper than the depth of the largest of the bulbs and wide enough so that several of the little mothers could to be put together with a bulb or two's width between them. I looked at them, fat and passive, content to live their lives of endless reproduction, and I sank to my knees on the wet grass.

They disgusted me.

A clammy dampness soaked through my skirt and chilled my knees as one by one I laid the bulbs out on the dark mattress of earth. I arranged them in two rows at first, like beds in a hospital ward, until a piece of chalky stone, turned up by the trowel, appeared among the rows like a doctor making his rounds. Then I broke up the two lines and laid the helpless bulbs out at random, where they sat, waiting for the comforting weight of earth to close over them like a shadow.

I don't know how long I knelt there, growing more drowsy, looking at the bulbs and wondering which of their tight, translucent skins would split open first, and when it did what kind of plant would be first to emerge.

The watery November light began to fade. I saw the rectangle of yellow light falling on the lawn and thought of the children tucked up in bed. Like them I too grew sleepy. The fistful of fat bulb-like pills that I had shaken from the bottle and planted with so little care in my own body were already beginning to flower, their anaesthetising tendrils snaking over nerve and vein, and my head grew heavy.

Hurriedly now I folded the dark blanket of soil back over the plump little forms, swaddling them in the furry darkness for which they longed. I patted the earth until it lay still and flat, like water closing over a sinking stone and, fighting the urge to puke, I lay my cheek against its cool surface and closed my eyes.

Rousing myself, I lifted my face from the soil and hastily now I began to plant the remaining groups of smaller bulbs, in shallower holes, allowing as much space again between each sleeper. Once or twice, when I could not tell a bulb's top from its bottom, I laid it gently on its side hoping to spare mother and child the pain of an inverted birth.

When I had finished it was dark. Somewhere in the garden I could hear the rustling of the brown paper bag. Groggy now, on my hands and knees I searched for it, but it had gone, carried by the evening breeze to settle out of reach among the roses. I climbed to my feet and then dragged my unwilling limbs back into the house. In the kitchen I passed the note I had propped between the salt and pepper pots and I paused before the cellar door. Unsteadily I slipped off my shoes and barefoot I padded down the stairs into the darkness below. On a pile of old carpet, smelling of turpentine and damp earth, I lay down and felt the barricades of sleep rise up between me and the outside world.

Above me the dim bulb in the kitchen drew long furrows of light between the floorboards, as though the tines of a rake were passing through the darkness overhead. I pulled the carpet over my face and the bright furrows disappeared from view. And like a penny dropped into a well, I sank deeper into the darkness, pressed down into the earth by unseen hands bedding me in for winter.

And I slept.

Weeding by Hand

with Émile Zola

TOOLS:
Trowel
Fork
Hoe
Hammer
Sickle

The last year of his life old Bonnemort had lain in his bed as the breath rattling through his rotten teeth grew shorter and more laboured and death patiently spread its tendrils through the old man's decaying body. For twelve full months the old miner's trowel and hoe had hung untouched on the back of the shed door, until the day that a fit of coughing came so violent that little streams of spittle, as black as pitch, ran down the sides of his mouth to gather like tar pits in the white hollows above his collar bone and Madame Bonnemort finally took down the key to her husband's shed and handed it to their lodger, Étienne.

Now the old man was dead and buried and it was Étienne who stood with the trowel in his calloused hand as he looked at the little parcel of land, so densely colonised that not one inch of earth could be seen through the labyrinthine thatch of weeds and grasses with which nature had reclaimed the ground as its own.

Stems of fennel, long since turned to seed, rose up from this battlefield like the tattered banners of a vanquished army, outnumbered and overwhelmed by the hordes of thistle and dandelion that had breached old Bonnemort's defences. Nearby a few spindly leaves of rocket could be seen, struggling still to hold out beneath a blanket of bindweed and ivy over which ranks of bramble and chickweed advanced, smothering the life from the old man's crops as surely as the pit dust had smothered the air in his lungs.

Every day since the old man's death Étienne had come here from his shift at the pit, to trowel and to hoe, to fork and to dig, labouring to ease the burden of weeds that lay like the yoke of capitalism on this little patch of ground. At first the tools seemed strange to him, but he expected to get used to them and to become attuned to the rhythms and tasks of his new life above ground as he had grown used to the work of the mine in the tunnels below. It was in the trowel work that he suffered the most. Crawling on the baked ground he struggled to control the long blade in the heavy soil, frightened each time he worked to expose the long tap root of a dandelion or a dock that the root would break, knowing that where one weed had grown now there would be two, or three, each fragment capable of regenerating itself into a full grown plant as voracious as its parent for earth and light and water.

Moving about the beds on planks, Étienne did his best to compact the soil as little as possible, but however carefully he made his way through the unwanted vegetation, great clouds of seed and pollen flew up, carried on the air to settle wherever they fell and begin again the process of germination. Overhead seeds of sycamore, spinning earthwards, fell like poison rain, seeding the ground with thrusting young saplings that threatened, if unchecked, to become a forest. Demoralised, he watched this army of seedlings mobilising in such numbers that at times he imagined he could feel them germinating in the ground beneath him, readying themselves to burst up from the depths and overrun the earth.

In no time patches of dried blood drew tattoos on the backs of his hands, and welts of white flesh, raised by the nettles that whipped back and forth in front of his eyes, scarred his face. After long hours spent crawling on the hard ground, the flesh of his palms and knees grew raw and tender, forcing him to abandon the trowel and take up the garden fork. Then the sound of his clogs rang out, striking the tines of the fork like a bell as he set to work among the brambles. With an obstinate resistance the powerful flora clung to the earth, forcing him to dig deeper until the white roots of the plants lay bare in the broken ground. Only then, his back crying out under the strain, did he stoop to pull at their thorn-free fixings, so reluctant to give up this land that they had claimed as their own.

These plants that had crushed the life out of the once flourishing rows of lettuce and radish, courgette and cauliflower, seemed now to Étienne no less hard than the pitiless coal face on which he had seen so many men broken. The dull ache of hunger began to grip his empty belly but when he looked about him for something to eat his eyes were met only with the dense wall of undergrowth that rose up from the parched earth. Chewing on the bitter leaf of a dandelion, he saw that he was not alone. He saw that the earth itself was dying of starvation as it laboured to feed the million roots and rhizomes that pierced its flesh, and his heart sank. How greedy they all were, he thought. How pitilessly they clutched at the earth, sucking the goodness from every grain of soil, leaving nothing on which to raise the fragile plants and seedlings that he hoped might one day feed him.

From time to time neighbours and colleagues from the pit called by, to watch him work or to give advice. Some came just to make fun of his efforts. "That's the way," encouraged Harel, the school teacher. "Do your weeding while the weather's hot and dry; it makes the weeds shrivel faster and will give them less chance of clinging on."

Even la Levaque, the barmaid, eyeing him mischievously as her breasts hung over the fence, had a word of advice for him. "The old man has done you no favours. Look at those dandelion clocks ready to drop. Haven't you heard, 'One year seed, seven years weed'? I can think of better things you could be doing with your time." Her coarse laughter echoed off the side of the old shed, making her breasts shake like dumplings boiling in a pot. But Étienne had no time.

"You're wasting your life," said Souvarine, the anarchist. "Look at the pollen rising. Every disturbance just increases your servitude. I expected better of you. Why don't you burn the lot?" But Étienne had not yet the stomach for revolution, nor did he share Souvarine's conviction that all plants are equal. He believed still that by peaceful means the good plants could be freed from the tyranny of the bad.

When he grew tired of their advice and could stand no more the glaring heat of the sun, the gardener withdrew into the shade of old Bonnemort's shed. Already Étienne had grown tired of the tyranny he had found on the allotment, where his new masters demanded even more of him than those in the mine. Sick with fatigue, he looked about him at the squalor of the old man's cabin. Baskets of tools and twine kept company with piles of terracotta pots; string bags filled with withered bulbs hung over seed trays labelled lettuce, spinach, green beans; seedlings all long past watering now lay dead and dried, like specimens in an apothecary's shop. On a shelf littered with the debris of the old gardener's life, a near-empty jar of sunflower seed caught his eye. Greedily he filled his mouth with its contents. Étienne then began poking among the dusty cans and bottles that crowded the shelves above, reading the labels written shakily in the old man's hand: coffee, sugar, weed killer, tomato feed, fertiliser. His hunger quelled by the excitement of these discoveries, the exhausted gardener began to dream. Was it possible that one of these containers held the secret of the succulent cabbages with which old Ma Bonnemort made her choucroutes and coleslaws? Could escape from the back-breaking cycle of labour be waiting at the bottom of a bottle?

For the first time he saw that the enemy was not the bosses, nor the mine owners and stockholders with their constant pursuit of profit, nor the citizens and their demand for lower prices, but nature herself; the nature that drove men to relive the sorrows of their fathers, the tragic marrow that lived in the bone. Numb with fatigue, the words of Souvarine echoing in his head, he felt sick at heart at the thought of beginning to weed again; it was too unfair, too hard. His human pride rebelled at the idea of becoming a slave to this patch of ground and he made up his mind. What was needed now was something cataclysmic. The anarchist had been right; a gardener must be prepared to wipe out everything and begin anew. Étienne looked again at the shelves of weed killers, uncertain of which to use. Weed killers that were to be painted onto the leaves of unwanted plants; weed killers that were to be soaked into the soil; selective weed killers that targeted only certain species. Looking at the contents of the cans one white powder looked much like another. Finally he made his decision. He would use them all.

Rapidly now, he began to combine the contents of all the jars and canisters into one lethal mixture, a fatal cocktail that was intended to wipe out tyranny and oppression once and for all. So impatient for his liberation was he that Étienne did not even notice that one of the cans held not weed killer, but sugar, the same sugar that old man Bonnemort had used to sweeten his coffee.

The sun climbed higher, beating down with increasing force on the little tin roof until the heat in the cabin had grown unbearable. Drowsily Étienne added the last of the ingredients to the deadly cocktail and crammed a lid onto the can. Then, gasping for air, his eyelids trembling in the glare of the sun, he staggered from the cabin. Dragging his heavy feet through the undergrowth, the exhausted gardener surrendered to the snares of bindweed and ivy and allowed himself to be pulled down into the tall grasses. He lay there and thought again of the old man until, overcome by the sun, under the swaying heads of creeping thistle, among the couch grass and horsetail, he dozed off.

When Étienne awoke the sun had passed its zenith. Groggily he sat up. His back was wet through, soaked with sweat and the bitter emanations of the leaves crushed beneath him, making his skin itch and burn. Insects buzzed about his ears. Through the nodding spires of buddleia only the roof of old Bonnemort's shed was visible. Patched with salvaged sheets of tin, it seemed to glow as though it had just been forged, the whole resembling nothing more than a miner's billycan simmering slowly in the heat of the sun. Bleary-eyed, parched with thirst, Étienne took up his trowel and headed back to the little cabin in which he had earlier mixed the potion that was to put an end to his labours. As he put his foot on the first step he noticed that the buzzing of the insects had suddenly stopped.

Etienne was on the top step when the door of old Bonnemort's cabin came off its hinges. Narrowly the door missed him, but the ball of flame that swept from the cabin enveloped him completely, instantly drying the sweat from his soaked clothes and burning the hair from his face and head. Thrown high by the force of the explosion, Étienne's limp body landed back in the vegetable patch, crushing the last surviving stems of rocket and parsley, and knocking the wind from his inflamed lungs with such severity that it was some moments before he could breathe again. When finally, his body shuddering back into life, he was able to suck in the hot air through his scorched lips, his nostrils were filled with the scent of his own burnt flesh. The trowel, knocked from his hand, was flung from one end of the allotment to the other and remained where it landed, in a clump of stinging nettles that covered what had once been an onion patch. Of the unwanted plants, a few had their leaves scorched by the explosion, but Étienne's body had taken most of the blast and the majority felt only a gust of hot air carrying their seed higher and farther than before. The few weeds that were burnt soon grew back. Etienne's hair, however, did not; not on his head nor on his chin. His scarred and sensitive skin, he found, was happiest in the darkness, and when his injuries were healed it was to the darkness that he returned, resuming his work in the mine. For the rest of his life the miner never forgot his experiences on the allotment and if ever any of his colleagues were heard to complain about the conditions underground, Étienne's white face could be seen laughing in the shadows. "Count your blessings," was his cry. "Cut coal doesn't grow back in a season."

Caring for Heather

with Alan Bennett

TOOLS:
Secateurs
Acidic soil
Good drainage

Heather began her career in the window box of number 23 The Avenue, Morecambe, Lancashire. Although much was made of her Scottish ancestry, number 23 was, in fact, the closest she came to travelling north of the border, having been raised from seed in the Wyevale nursery just off the A26 outside Cleethorpes. A window box is perhaps not the most promising of beginnings for a plant, but nevertheless it was one that introduced her early in life to the rigours of playing front of house and kept her from the more sedentary pleasures of providing ground cover in the mixed border for the rest of her career.

As chance would have it, the owner of number 23, Mr

Crofton, still living with his Scottish mother though he must have been well into his fifties even then, was the head gardener for the local council and as such was also responsible for the plant display that faced on to the seafront's crowning glory, the Variety Theatre. Well it happened that late one evening, the star of the show, leaving the theatre after playing a near empty house and one too many drinks in his dressing room, fell vomiting into the ornamental bed. Though the name of the actor escapes me, I still recall how, with unanimous verdict, the ladies at the bus stop agreed he was "a disgusting pig", a term coined first by my mam as she listened to the story told by Mr Crofton's mother, with whom we were waiting for the 96 bus.

Having been diagnosed as polluted beyond the realms of decency, the injured plants were removed, and Mr Crofton found himself, at short notice, in need of a performer who could cope with the now acidic soil and could also be counted on to suppress the weeds that will naturally fill any vacancy in a flower bed. Heather was at hand and a career was launched. She was still playing the seafront in various roles almost a decade later. Heather had a glorious season in 2005 when, in what must have been her busiest year ever, she appeared in no fewer than five displays, including a floral tribute to soldiers serving overseas, a fund-raising parterre for the RNLI and a final show-stopping appearance in the town's floral clock. Mr Crofton, still the borough's plantsman-in-chief, had cast Heather in a small supporting role for which, after considerable coaching and pruning, she was to represent the numeral 2 in what was to be the centrepiece of Morecambe's floral attractions that year. His ailing mother now suffering from dementia, Mr Crofton had left the maintenance of the clock to his young assistant and he, more used to dealing with the softer foliage of pansies and pelargoniums, had overlooked the mid-spring prune to which Heather was so partial, and although this required no more than a quick flourish of the shears to remove Heather's flowers as soon as they died back, a sort of horticultural shampoo and set, it also served to prevent her growth becoming too leggy. As a result, within a month, at ten minutes past four on a Thursday afternoon, the clock's minute hand became entrapped in Heather's woodier growth. The resulting late start to the entertainments on the bandstand and the failure of a group of elderly French tourists to rejoin their coach on time, not to mention the consequent missed ferry, was newsworthy enough to make the local papers and within a week Heather found herself removed from the display in what must have been humiliating circumstances.

Insult was added to injury when, in his haste to cut her free, Mr Crofton's well-meaning junior inadvertently cut into Heather's old wood, leaving an unsightly brown patch from which she never flowered again. Thus disfigured she was put into storage, in a grow bag of ericaceous compost at the municipal nursery. It must have seemed to Heather that her career was over; until the following spring, when Mr Crofton, finding himself short of a gift on Mother's Day, had Heather potted up. Then, with a tartan bow tied neatly around her container, he drove her over to the nursing home in neighbouring Heyshel. After a distressing twenty minutes being mistaken for his ninety-three-year-old mother's chiropodist, Mr Crofton left Heather balanced on top of the television set where she cut a lonely figure in this, the last stage of her career, as a rather unkempt and misshapen figure 2. And when later the increasingly confused Mrs Crofton began asking staff if it was her second birthday, it was thought best to remove Heather to the communal lounge. And so, in the twilight of her career, Heather found herself topping the bill on the window sill in the south-facing lounge of the Elmbourne nursing home.

Heather's real name was *Erica cinerea*, a name she found somewhat too exotic for her Lancashire public. She was not one for flashy display. Long before the current trend for banana trees and exotic grasses Heather had been a favourite in the rockeries that were so popular in her youth, her love of direct sun and tolerance of drought being just two of the qualities that made her so popular. So it was no surprise to me that she approached this last engagement with such professionalism, seeing no shame in the ordinariness of this final playhouse, nor in the drowsiness of this, her last audience, in whose watery gaze she might have glimpsed not just admiration, but also affection, the residents mistaking Heather's unruly mop on more than one occasion for a long-lost pet or rarely seen grandchild peering in at the window.

It was with no little sadness that I saw Heather for the last time while visiting my own mother in Elmbourne Rest Home just a few weeks before Heather passed away. By then Heather had lost the pink lilac colouring on which her reputation had been made, most of her flowers having long since dropped, and I imagine that many of her fans would have had great difficulty in recognising her as the young lass that had been such a hit in those early days on Morecambe seafront.

Knowing she loved to be in the sun, one of the staff had positioned her above a radiator, on a window sill so hot on sunny days that you could have boiled an egg on it. That wouldn't have bothered Heather so much as the lack of fresh air to which she had always been partial. And though Heather liked a drink, one of her many merits as a house plant was that she never minded being passed over by the watering can, a trait that must have caused her no end of suffering during the summer season at Morecambe, where rain topped the bill as often, if not more so, than sun. What finished her off in the end was too much water. When it came to plant care the approach at Elmbourne could best be described as feast or famine, and when one of the younger members of staff, noticing Heather's compost had dried out, stood her to soak stem-deep in a Tupperware salad bowl, the end was nigh. Hardly the ideal conditions for a plant of her temperament. By the time I reached her it was too late. There were bluish-black stains on her branches, and beneath the voluminous skirts of her foliage ominous patches of decay were beginning to spread up the base of her stem.

She had succumbed to what gardeners describe as chlorotic leaf and root rot, old age being an unacceptable diagnosis in these politically correct times. But ten years is a pretty good innings for a shrub of her sort. Before I left, the manager of the home remarked on what an undemanding resident Heather had been. "We've had ornaments here that have needed more attention than that Heather. Wherever we put her she made the best of it," he said, unintentionally summing up the attitude of many an institution towards its older residents, not dissimilar to that of a lost property office towards forgotten parcels.

Caring for Heather

In the end there was a strange symmetry to a career that had its beginning on one side of a window pane coming to its end on the other, and a more fitting place for the curtain to come down, than on a window sill, I can't imagine.

Erica cinerea, 1996–2006

Propagating from a Vine

with Mary Shelley

INGREDIENTS:
Cuttings compost
Fungicide
Vine or climber

It was a stormy night in August when I put down my travelling case and stepped again into the humid gloom of the potting shed. There, as the rain pattered dismally against the panes overhead, amid the scent of wet loam and cedar I first beheld the accomplishment of my toil.

How shall I describe the wretched creeper whose propagation ought to have been the crowning glory of so many infinite pains and cares? Animated by a convulsive motion, the strange Nepalese vine had grown with an ardour unimaginable, so that now its coils appeared to have overwhelmed every surface and upright of the humble outhouse in which for so long and with so little success my profane fingers had disturbed the secrets of the bindweed and the honeysuckle. Proof positive that I had finally succeeded in discovering the cause of propagation, nay more, I had become capable of bestowing animation upon a lifeless cutting. No father could claim more delight and rapture than I on first seeing his creation, nor understand more fully how my rapture turned to loathing, when by the glimmer of the half extinguished candle, I perceived the extraordinary sight (sight tremendous and abhorred) that greeted my arrival. What ought to have been my Adam had become rather my fallen angel, fallen with a vengeance, starving its neighbours of light and moisture, of air and space, strangling its brethren one by one, until alone the serpentine and unnatural vine held dominion over the potting shed.

How I came to make this breakthrough I will tell you. Learn from me how dangerous is the propagation of the unknown, how unhappy the gardener whose search for glory takes him beyond the borders set by nature.

In the pursuit of my studies it was my habit to spend long hours rooting in the compost heaps of my neighbourhood, seeking amongst death and decay the answer to the mysteries of plant propagation. Here I beheld the corruption of decay succeed to the shining surface of the leaf, here I learnt how quickly the blindworm takes possession of the petal of blossom and bloom and here too I saw with what distasteful haste mould inherited the rosehip and the cucumber. From such pits of putrefaction I salvaged the lumps of green flesh with which I would return to my potting shed, where, confident in the ultimate success of my undertaking, I planted them, sheltered from the scorching of the sun, nourished by the primordial peat.

As summer came on, the steaming heaps from which I drew my grotesque specimens became increasingly overwhelmed with grass clippings, swamping all else in a green slime that accelerated the process of decay, until for my specimens I came to depend on those brought to my door by students and colleagues familiar with the purpose of my studies.

Among these callers there came one night a dark-skinned man, his head covered and dressed after the manner of the hillsmen of the Himalayas. In his hands he held a length of vine, a piece of cord, I might have thought, in the hands of an assassin, were it not for the leafy couplets which interrupted its length. The cutting had most likely been taken earlier that evening, stolen, I didn't doubt, from the garden of his employer. I paid the fellow what he asked, and took the cutting directly to my laboratory, or potting shed as you might call it.

Seeing the stem was in excellent condition, I was moved to attempt for one last time an experiment I had tried earlier that year without success. I first removed the leaves from a length of vine and then, with the aid of a sharp blade, wounded the underside of the stem, scraping the epidermis with the edge of a knife so as to expose the watery green core. I then placed the injured limb in a trench no wider or deeper than a man's finger, covered it with earth and generously humidified the area with a fungicide of my own preparation.

The hour was late and since it was to be my last night at the house for some time I closed the door of my laboratory and retired to prepare my bags for the following day, when I was to make my way south to spend a month hiking the Alpine pastures with my friend Henry Clerval. How I wish I had not taken up Henry's invitation, rejoicing in the salubrious Alpine air, oblivious to the monster taking shape in my own home amongst the unhallowed damps of the cold frame and the cloche. Now, nearly five weeks later, the demonic creeper to which I had so miserably given life had grown too vast to submit longer to the will of its creator.

While this vegetable devil destroyed the hopes of all its neighbours, still it could not satisfy its own desires, forever ardent and craving. Before me now, in the faint moonlight that broke through the dark and comfortless sky, I saw its blind buds, reaching even unto me, their creator, beckoning me closer, urging me to surrender myself into the life-sapping grip of a thousand tendrils. Where for so long I had pursued nature into her hiding places, now she pursued me, inviting me to find oblivion in its deadly caress and in so doing purge myself of self-loathing and guilt. Overcome by my own sin, the hubris of the gardener who in seeking glory fails to pay homage to the one true Creator, I yielded. And with a cry that set the panes of the greenhouse atremble, I threw myself into its waiting coils, ready for its crushing grip to strip the life from my lungs.

Repotting a House Plant

with Martin Amis

HORTICULTURAL AIDS:
Plant pot
Compost
Drainage material
Water — still or sparkling

You'll probably guess, before even my composted memory can retrace the events, that this is the story of a gardener, a sub-urban sward cutter, a Home Counties fuschia fancier, who finds himself far from home and in search of thrills. It's also the story of a prisoner, or a hostage at least, and a liberation. But however far you may take the gardener out of suburbia, you won't take suburbia out of the gardener.

My body is a dictionary. A dictionary of pain. From my arse to my zygotic nerve it hurts. It hurts a lot. There are earth stains on my shirt, on the bed. Rinds of dirt press insistently under my fingernails as though I've spent the night clawing my way free of a premature burial. God, I hate mornings, the endless succession of questions posed by my ageing body, that endless succession of surprises and pain as memory begins to taunt me and the first messages begin coming in from witnesses of the night before, checking to see if I am still alive.

My mouth is like a swarm of bees that only smoke will calm. I take a packet of Downhill from the bedside table and light the first of the day. On the match fold, beneath the silhouette of a woman leaning provocatively against a palm tree, the legend Palms Lounge, its thermographed lettering straining against the confines of the flat surface, provides memory with her first opening and she hits me with a darting left jab to my paper-thin temple. The blow has shaken me. I'm a little unsteady on my feet as I stand, tightening the belt of my robe across the boulder of my gut, to call down to the desk for coffee. "For one or two?" says the desk clerk knowingly.

"For six," I say. "On second thoughts send me all you've got."

A rangy bellboy with an Adam's apple like a three-pound tumour puts down the tray of coffee. I watch his sleepy eyes widen in surprise at the sight of my loamy digits dismissing him with a tip. As I pour the first of the peat-brown liquid into the cup, memory strikes again. A combination this time. Left to the ribs. Right to the head and then a left to the gut. When I pick my crumpled jacket from the floor I can feel the heavy bulk pulling it out of shape. The rubberised grip is sticky in my hand as I lift the heavy instrument from the pocket and lay it on the table. And now, seeing my guard drop, memory unleashes a powerful right. My head snaps back, my gum shield flies from my loosening teeth and I fall to the canvas. Fight over. I look up. From the table top the stainless blade of a garden trowel glints painfully in the morning light. It's all coming back to me. I won't be going back to Palms Lounge in a hurry, that's for sure.

While the first pint of coffee osmoses into my bloodstream and the compost of coffee grounds sits steaming at the bottom of my cup, I light another Downhill and begin running over the events of the day before. The contract signed, drinks, lunch, more drinks. The taxi to Palms Lounge. My colleagues whooping when the hostess greets me by name. Don't mock. I had a month to spend on my own in this city, I'd already spent an evening deadheading the rosebush outside my hotel. Twice I'd stayed late at the office to replant the necropolitan window boxes that blighted the views from every window. Gardening opportunities being limited after dark, what else was I going to do?

Located on the eastern fringe of the financial district, the Palms Lounge is a gentlemen's club. Like most gentlemen's clubs it doesn't see many gentlemen. Beered-up lawyers and rat-arsed accountants looking for low-rent nights to escape their high-rent lives are the backbone of the club's clientele. The lounge itself is a cramped basement in which everything that is not painted black is brown. Miles of exposed trunking and pipework zigzag back and forth across the walls and ceiling, carrying services no doubt to the fluorescent green office block that stands on the site above ground. Within their labyrinthine growth, the club's faux-leather furniture is clustered around a tiny stage like fat beetles in the gloom, on whose easy-wipe surfaces the patrons of the club gather, happy to take part in the club's fucked-up parlour games for pissed-up priapists.

Repotting a House Plant

After four weeks of coming to this place, four weeks of leering over Tilly Palmer's silicon valleys, four weeks of watching Hedda Foremen's irrepressible thighs threatening to burst the banks of their stocking tops, I'd begun to develop a healthy contempt for the scummy clientele who frequent this gloomy burrow. Not because of their shabby treatment of the syphilitic sirens bending over backwards to show them a good time, but because of their abject failure to acknowledge the plight of the pot-bound palms that sit dying on every table of this C-list flesh pot and meatery. I pick up the example in front of me and show it to my colleague, Stock Byers. Having out-grown their diminutive domain, its centipede-like roots protruded from the bottom of the pot, venturing forth pre-sumably in search of channels of grime in which to feed. "Look at that, it's a fucking disgrace. Whoever's in charge of these ought to be sacked."

"They're sagging a bit, sure, but man, look at her move. I wouldn't say no." Stock wasn't looking at the plant. His eyes were fixed instead on the gyrations of dancer number six, the concentric motion of her surgical augmentations apparently holding his sodden brain in a state of deep hypnosis. I pressed my thumb into the compost. Beneath the granite-like crust that had formed on its surface the potting material was dry and spent.

"There's no nutrients left in here, this thing needs repotting."

I raised my hand. Within seconds a shop-soiled hostess had stacked her pencil-thin thighs across my knees. "Dance for you, Mr Gardner?" she said, placing, with jejune charm, a slen-der hand against the inside of my thigh.

"No. Fetch me some water." Disappointment flashed across her face, but her response was automatic.

"Sparkling or still?"

"Do you think this thing gives a fuck?" I held the plant up to her face. "Two bottles of it. And bring me an ice bucket, *no ice*, and a corkscrew."

While I waited for the return of my sulky water carrier I watched Stock. Like two sunflowers tracking the approaching sun, his wide eyes followed Tilly's transit. Gripping the arms of his chair, he was craning forwards, his every feature beseeching the hot flesh upon the stage to engulf him in its sordid warmth. When his call was answered she came upon him like a storm. Stock's face met Tilly's churning breasts head-on as they began to break like waves upon the bows of his cheeks, her ferocious back-lit hair lashing the decks of his thinning scalp, until, like a storm at sea, she withdrew. Momentarily Stock's head held its position before plunging forward, his storm-swept forehead shattering his plate as it hit the table.

"What's a matter with him?" The water nymph had returned. She snapped the twenty-dollar bill into the taut darkness of her stocking top and watched as I poured the first of the San Badino *slightly sparkling* onto the plant that I had now identified as a *Dracaena fragrans*, *Dracaena fragrans moribunda* to give it its full name.

"He's fine," I said. "He likes his food." Unwilling to be sidetracked by her concern for my comatose colleague, I stepped up to the coat check and presented my token. On the fifth attempt the attendant succeeded in hoisting the seventy-litre sack of compost onto the counter. I dropped a quarter into the gratuities saucer and dragged my reclaimed dirt back to where the ailing *Dracaena*, having drunk its fill, was now sitting in a pool of its own earthy piss.

I lay the soggy-footed plant on its side and gave its pot a series of hefty slaps. A fibrous whirlpool of spent dirt and wizened root fell onto the table top, its arachnoid tendrils sucking on the ball of starved earth like a spider feeding on a long-dead fly. Doing my best not to damage the tiny filaments through which the plant had been drawing its scant sustenance, I teased the starving roots away from the pathetic little earth ball and with a butter knife cut back some of the longer outgrowths.

Another dancer had taken over from the snake-eyed Tilly. I recognised her. It was Hedda Foremen. She was hanging from a pole, looking out through the obscene bifurcation formed by her raised and parted legs, as though through the sights of some huge gun. With a shudder I remembered the three hundred bucks I'd offered her to come back to my hotel two nights before. Pondering the frankness of her refusal and the cleft in her pants, I picked up the corkscrew and used it to bore a hole in the bottom of the champagne bucket. No one was watching. Their priapic virilia safely fastened beneath their zipper trelliswork, the pot-bound punters were ogling Hedda. By the time she'd slithered down from her pole, I was already sweeping the fragments of broken crockery from around Stock's face into my newly bored planter. For once, as Hedda's powerful thighs began their advance across the dance floor, I wasn't paying attention. I was crouched over the open bag of compost. With an empty champagne glass I was scooping dollops of black soil onto the drainage material so conveniently provided by Stock's broken plate. Then, easing the palm's roots once more out of their foetal cringe, I placed them in the pot and began draping them in a velvet cloak of black compost. When only the palm's leaves could be seen, I patted the compost down and gave the plant a thorough soaking with the second bottle of San Badino. Almost immediately a carbonated slurry began draining from the bucket towards the edge of the table where Hedda's buttocks, recently arrived, were waiting to touch down next to Stock's catatonic countenance. When I looked up it was just in time to see her chiffon-clad cheeks damming the course of the dirty brook. Hedda looked round, aware that her concentration had been broken by the unpleasant sensation of something cold and wet soaking into her pants. Leaping up, she wheeled round and stood glaring at me as her soiled underwear dripped into the puddle that was forming on the floor. Instinctively I raised my glass. It was filled with John Innes No. 2 Compost. My gallant gesture was misinterpreted. "What is it with perverts like you?" Other punters were craning forward now, struggling to see the form of my particular perversity. Seeing the dark puddle in which the furious dancer stood screaming, someone in the crowd called out, "Hey, Hedda, did you shit your pants?" His gallant remark did little to calm the situation. With a roar Hedda turned on me. Lunging across the table she knocked the glass from my hand, and what she would have done next I will never know, for at that moment her stratospheric heels lost their balance. On the wet floor her lunge became a skitter. Her legs racing like a flicker book, she grabbed in desperation at the table's edge. Like the last moments of the Titanic, the table pitched upright: bottles, glasses, cellphones, Stock's head, all slid towards the cadent dancer. All except for the *Dracaena*. That I had saved, and through its variegated foliage I watched as another burst of strobe lighting rendered the final moments of Hedda's crash in slow motion. For an eternity she seemed to hang in the air, then the strobe cut out and she fell.

The upturned table had been enough to wake Stock from his coma. A fragment of broken crockery was still sticking to his forehead when he raised his face and saw Hedda. "I thought you said she didn't go down?" he said. The next thing I remember was the sound of doors opening, closing, the fresh air on my face, my arms held like handles by the two gorillas who replanted me on the street. Two heavy thuds as Stock and the near-full bag of compost were dumped alongside me. Where they are now I have no idea. The last I remember was flinging a fistful of bills into the driver's greasy hand as I stepped from a cab. In the back seat Stock was sleeping like a baby, his head nestled on a pillow of compost. He had the same look of contentment on his grubby face that he wore when Hedda's breasts enveloped him in their milky squall. If the money's not run out they're probably both still there. Turning in circles about the city. Those clubs are all the same, full of men who've forgotten how much they need their Mother Earth.

How to Prune the Rose

with Pablo Neruda

TOOLS:
Secateurs
Courage
Love

I have named you queen,
My sleeping one.
At winter's approach I have watched you grow drowsy
Falling into a sleep that deepens
With each passing day.
While I, your summer lover
Who spent long afternoons
And late nights by your side,
Drinking in your perfume,
Am left behind.
When I approach you now, it is not with a kiss,
But with a blade in my hands.
Forgive me my love. You must,

How to Prune the Rose

For I am the guardian of our love.
Before I sleep I will cut away your deadwood,
Your damaged branches,
Your crossing and congested stems will I remove.
So that you will not wound yourself in the troubled dreams
that come
When the north wind shakes your boughs.
Free flowing air will circulate among your stems
And no disease will trouble your rosy limbs.
Each cut is kind,
The blades close tight above the bud
Whose growth will make your figure fair
In summers yet to come.
I angle my secateurs upwards
With each diagonal cut an oval of fleshy white pith appears.
They hang about your body like moonstones.

How shocked I am at what I have done.
You stand, my love, barely a foot from the ground
Your leaves all gone now, clad only in a coat of thorns
With which you prick and scratch at me
And I feel myself alone once more.
And I too long for winter to wrap me in its cloak of ether
To sleep knowing, deep in my own white pith, that you will
wake me in the spring.
With your first blood-red bloom you will summon me to
your side
And our love will live again.